ESTONIA: Nation on the Anvil

ESTONIA: Nation on the Anvil

by Emanuel Nodel

BOOKMAN ASSOCIATES, INC.
New York 3, N. Y.

Dedication

To my Mother and my Wife, who helped me through life, and without whose love and encouragement this work would never have been completed. In love and appreciation

E. N.

Preface

This book is the fulfillment of an idea cherished during my undergraduate days at the Estonian State University in Tartu. Studying Estonian history and literature, I was struck by an interesting phenomenon in the development of the Estonian people: the amazingly fast transformation of the Estonian peasants, who only one generation ago had no distinct national consciousness of their own, into a nationally proud people. Such a speedy development aroused not only my admiration but also my curiosity and influenced my future historical interest greatly. The presence of the so-called *Kadakasaksad* * ("Juniper Germans"), *i.e.,* Germanized Estonians, an atavism from the not distant past, was a living witness to the quondam slave-psychology of the Estonian peasants. At the same time, the existence of those few *Kadakasaksad* emphasized the tremendous change through which the Estonian peasants had passed, managing by their own strength to break the barriers of ignorance and lack of self-respect and attain a mature, independent culture.

The smallness of Estonia and the agrarian character of its people, where about seventy-five per cent of the population lived on farms, gave me ample opportunity during my high school and university years to observe the people in their daily work, in their cultural and social activities. From the city to the country was only a very short distance—emotionally as well as physically—especially during the summer months, which most of the Estonian youth spent on farms. It was from this experience that I became aware of the miraculous transformation of the Estonian people. I realized that the historic process of the evolution of the Estonian peasant was not yet over, since I could still feel the breath of the past.

7

Presented with this view of history-in-the-making, I became absorbed by the problem: what factors caused the growth of Estonian national consciousness from its obscure beginnings in the 1860's until the birth of the Estonian state during the First World War?

For a better understanding of this historical development, I decided to begin with the aftermath of the Great Northern War and trace the economic, social, and cultural development of the Estonian people up to the present time. During the years 1939-1941 I collected materials on this problem with the ultimate goal of publishing my conclusions as a Master's thesis. The outbreak of the German-Russian war in June, 1941, stopped me at the very beginning of its realization.

Years later, while a graduate student at Indiana University I was very fortunate in finding material for this book. In the Baltic Collection, purchased by the University Library in 1952, I found enough material to continue my interrupted research. There is, however, a great difference between the sources I had at my disposal in Estonia, and those at Indiana University. In Estonia I accumulated German, Russian, and Estonian materials which represented an even balance of the points of view of the three national schools of historiography concerning the process of Estonian emancipation. In the Indiana University Baltic Collection, on the other hand, I found mostly Germany books and periodicials representing the German point of view, with few Russian or Estonian materials. The hundreds of documents on which my dissertation is based are overwhelmingly pro-German, and very few present the Estonian point of view objectively. This collection, moreover, proved inadequate to enable me to trace the growth of Estonian national consciousness after 1907 up to the First World War, as I had originally intended. The chronological scope of my survey has necessarily, therefore, been cut down, and I have concluded the study with only a brief survey of the aftermath of the 1905 revolution. Confronted thus with sources representing mainly a negative approach to the history of Estonian emancipation, I have had the difficulty of developing a positive theory of the process. This has been my greatest handicap and I am fully aware of it.

This book does not pretend to be a history of the Estonian people from the Great Northern War until the 1905 revolution. Neither does it pretend to cover all the facts pertaining to the development of national consciousness of the Estonian people. What I have tried to do is to trace the relationship and attitude of the Baltic German nobility toward the emancipation of the Estonian people during the eighteenth and nineteenth centuries, and merely to record their negative as well as positive impact upon the growth of Estonian national consciousness.

TABLE OF CONTENTS

I   The Economic and Cultural Ruin of the Estonian Provinces during and after the Great Northern War and the Slow Process of Recuperation   13

II   Economic and Cultural Changes in Estonia during the Reign of Alexander I   29

III   The Failure of Liberalism and the End of the Manorial System   41

IV   The Beginnings of National Awakening   55

V   Urbanization, Agricultural Trends and Cultural Developments, 1830-1860   71

VI   Turning Points in the Development of Estonian National Consciousness and the Beginning of Internal Political Strife   79

VII   National Awakening and National Activities   93

VIII   Russification and the Decline of Militant Estonian Nationalism   111

IX   The Eve of the Revolution   123

X   The 1905 Revolution   135

XI   The Road to Freedom   159

Conclusion: The Estonian People—From the Aftermath of the 1905 Revolution Until the First Soviet Occupation   169

Notes   179

Bibliography   197

Index   205

CHAPTER I

The Economic and Cultural Ruin of the Estonian Provinces
during and after the Great Northern War and the Slow
Process of Recuperation

1. The Economic Situation of the Estonian Peasants after 1721 and the Perpetuation of Serfdom

During the nineteenth century the Estonian people went through great historical changes. Whereas at the beginning of the century they entirely lacked national consciousness, were chained in serfdom, culturally and politically ignorant, without a trace of their own literature, we find them at the beginning of the twentieth century a self-conscious people, with a culture and literature of their own and with a well-entrenched peasantry, middleclass and intelligentsia. How did this transformation occur within one century and what were the forces which fostered such progress?

The eighteenth century began with an event most fateful and disastrous for the Estonian people: the Great Northern War. This war caused the economic and cultural ruin of the Estonian provinces for almost a century to follow.[1] The destruction of many cities and villages and the great loss in population brought life almost to a complete stagnation.[2]

With the peace of Nystad in August, 1721, the Estonian provinces (Estonia and Northern Livonia) became a part of the Russian Empire. The Russian government granted to the Baltic Germans rights which they had enjoyed prior to the Northern War. Thus the power of the Baltic German nobility increased even more. Peter the Great granted them such rights as German courts, the use of German as the official language, and absolute control over the Protestant church in the Baltic provinces.[3]

Under Swedish rule the administration of the Baltic provinces became more and more centralized, with the power of the German nobility diminishing. The situation changed again in favor of the nobles after the country fell under Russian rule.[4] The new Russian governors were in most cases appointed from among the local German nobility; and even if the governor happened to be a Russian, he soon fell under German influence and acted according to the German interests. To increase their political power the nobles obtained from the Russian government a so-called Matriculation *(Matrikel)* book. In these *Matrikels* only those nobles were inscribed who belonged to the oldest families (about two hundred); and only these families enjoyed the full right to administer the country. In such a way the nobility made sure that they were the only rulers of the Baltic provinces with their power undiminished.

Though politically Estonia and Livonia were under Russian rule, culturally and religiously they were still close to Germany. The cultural contact was not interrupted by the Russian annexation. Owing to the lack of universities in the Baltic provinces, the nobles usually sent their sons into German universities or brought tutors from Germany.

While the position of the German nobility thus improved, the position of the Estonian population worsened steadily and reached its lowest point at the beginning of the nineteenth century. Under Russian rule the Baltic nobility received back those estates confiscated by the Swedes. The Estonian peasant lost all the privileges he had received from the Swedish king and became just as unprotected as the Russian peasant was—a serf without any rights.

The Estonian peasants had no right to own land, cattle, or any other property. They did not even have any rights over their own families, and could be sold separately by the baron without their consent like chattells or head of cattle. They had to pay many dues and taxes to the lords (in money and in services) and to the state; and in addition they had to support the church and the clergy.

Corporal punishment was part of the peasant's every-day life. Conditions became so bad that many peasants who lived on the northern shores of the Baltic provinces escaped by boat into Finland. In his article on "Peasant movements in Livonia" E. F. Dubiuk, a Soviet historian, writes:

The escape of the peasants from Livonia in 1765 became so obvious that even Catherine the Great knew about it. She wrote to a Russian resident in Courland, a certain Semionov, that it was known to her from previous denunciations of the governmental office in Riga that the number of escaped peasants from Livonia was so great that some localities became deserted.[5]

To meet this growing danger, the Tsarina began to show some interest in the improvement of rural conditions. She required the German nobles to transfer some of their land to the peasants and to put certain limitations to the latter's dues. At the beginning the nobles did not wish to accept Catherine's proposals. After being warned, however, that in cases of stubborn resistance the new regulations would come by decree, and after long deliberations, they finally agreed to grant to the peasants some small rights of ownership.

The legislation embodying these rights was announced to the peasants through the churches, but was not printed in the Estonian language or published through the countryside in written form. In practice, the new regulations did not change much of the peasant's life. Since the Russian government lacked any means of enforcing the regulations, they became merely dead letters.[6]

2. The Beginnings of Criticism of Serfdom: The Estophils

Though the majority of the nobility was zealous for the continuation of old forms of serfdom, there, nevertheless, appeared among the Germans in the eighteenth century men who protested against the medieval conditions prevailing in the Baltic provinces. The motives of these reformers varied; but they all believed that a change must be made if the peasants were not to be brought to the verge of economic collapse.

Among private tutors who came from Germany and among some German pastors were outstanding liberal-minded men, who became interested in the economic and cultural conditions of the Estonians (or Latvians).

The first among them was Johann Georg Eisen von Schwarzenberg (1717-1779) who was a clergyman in Torma and Lohusu, Estonia. Eisen published a book in which he demanded the improvement of economic conditions of the peasants, the limitation of serfdom, and the recognition of the right of peasants to own land. In his defence of the peasants Eisen showed that for the benefit of both the noblemen and peasantry the latter must be made free so they could be more productive.[7] That would make the economy of the country flourish and the peasants would rise culturally while improving economically. Eisen's book aroused hatred among the German nobility; but, having good connections in the imperial court in St. Petersburg, he could continue his enlightening activity among the nobility for a long time.

Of great importance for the emancipation of the peasants was Heinrich von Jannau (1753-1821), a German-speaking historian. Jannau was born in Holstre, Estonia. He studied theology in Göttingen, Germany, and became pastor in Põlva and Laius, in Estonia. Jannau showed great interest in public education. His works were of great importance for the enlightenment of his German contemporaries. In his *Sitten und Zeit, ein Memorial an Liev und Estland* (Riga, 1781) he criti-

cized the manners and life, as well as education, social activities, and religious life of the Baltic nobility. In his *Provinzial-
blätter an das Liev- und Ehstländische Publicum* (1786),
Jannau deplored the poverty and living standards of the
Estonian peasants, and he asked the nobles to change their
despotic attitude toward the peasants and treat them as
fathers should treat their children.

What was probably Jannau's most important work, *Geschichte der Sklaverei und Charakter der Bauern in Liefland
und Esthland*, published in 1786, found the greatest response
among the more enlightened and liberal Germans in the
Baltic provinces, as well as in the German states. In this book
Jannau described the origin and development of serfdom
and sharply denounced the institution, showing its bad influences upon the character of the Estonian peasant with
respect to drunkenness, thievery, and criminality. Jannau
accused the German nobility of having promoted among the
Estonian peasants such vices as drunkenness and thievery.
He demanded that the nobles give their peasants a legal position and promote their cultural growth so they would aban-
don bad customs and manners. Nevertheless, Jannau was
against an immediate abolition of serfdom as such, because
of the low cultural and moral level of the Estonians. The
peasants, he believed, should know their duties and rights,
which must be made clear in their native tongue. To improve
education to this end, he advised teaching the peasant children reading, writing, and arithmetic.

In his other work on Baltic history, *Geschichte von Lief-
und Ehstland pragmatisch vorgetragen* (1793), Jannau expressed a liberal view on Baltic history, criticizing strongly
the Baltic nobility for their selfish attitude toward their
peasants.

Eisen and Jannau were not the only liberals and human-
ists among a majority of feudal-minded nobles. One of them,
an outstanding humanist, linguist, and publicist was August
Wilhelm Hupel (1737-1819). Hupel was born in Germany,

where he early acquired enlightened views. Soon after graduation from the university of Jena, in 1754, he left for the Baltic provinces, where he settled in Riga (1757) as a private tutor.[8] After 1769 he moved into Estonia, where he spent the rest of his life in active social and literary work. Hupel became very interested in the life and habits of the Estonian peasants. He published many books in such diversified fields as the topography of Estonia, economics, and folklore, and also wrote an Estonian grammar.

Throughout his life Hupel mingled actively with the Estonian population, helping everybody as much as he could. In writing and speech, he always denounced serfdom and the cruelty of the nobility towards their peasants. Hupel's influence became very great throughout his life, especially among liberal-minded Germans. His works on his chosen country, Estonia, and his first Estonian grammar laid the foundations for further studies in the field of Estonian linguistics.[9]

Another great German liberal and humanist was Garlieb Merkel (1769-1850). Merkel was born in Estonia and brought up in great poverty. In his youth he was influenced by the liberal ideas of his father. Merkel was soon in contact with young nobles with whom he interchanged ideas whose origin could be found in the French Revolution. Observation of the situation of the Estonian and Latvian peasants developed in him an intense dislike for the institution of serfdom.

It was in Livonia that Merkel began writing his first book, *Die Letten Vofzüglich in Liefland am Ende des Philosophischen Jahrhunderts,* but he finished it in Leipzig, where it was published in 1800. Appearing at a time when the reformist ideas of the eighteenth century had exploded in the French Revolution and the old order was shaken throughout Europe, the work aroused great interest among the German public. Merkel sharply denounced the poverty of the peasants and the ugliness of serfdom. He showed how such a condition demoralized the peasants, and he demanded such reforms as the fixing of the peasants' payments in agricultural products and in labor. This work aroused great hatred among the Baltic nobility, and its circulation was forbidden in Livonia by the governor. Nevertheless, young German nobles read Merkel's book and were greatly influenced by it.

In another pamphlet called *Beweis dass es halb so viel koste seine Ländereien von Tagelöhnern bestellen zu lassen als von Leibeigenen Bauern* (1814), Merkel substantiated his attacks upon serfdom. In this, as in later works, the indefatigable writer pointed out the necessity of liberating the peasants from serfdom as a means of improving not only the peasant's lot, but also the economic structure and productivity of the country in general.

Merkel wrote, also, other books in defense of the emancipation of the peasants and stressed the absolute necessity of reforms in the Baltic provinces. Though he was not always accurate or balanced in describing conditions in Livonia, his books nevertheless influenced his contemporaries greatly and helped bring about a more humane treatment of the Baltic peasants. In the long run, they were doubtlessly one of the factors which led to eventual full emancipation.

A small beginning of the realization of the ideas of Jannau, Hupel, Eisen, and Merkel was made by a Baltic nobleman, Baron Karl Friedrich Schoultz of Ascheraden (1720-1782). Schoultz was a man not only of liberal views, but also of practical action and courage. From his own observations he realized the hopelessness of the economic order, and was fully aware of the unproductiveness of serf labor and the potential danger of poverty and despair among the peasants. He was the first to introduce on his estates reforms limiting the dues, fixing the labor-norms of the peasants, and granting the latter certain ownership rights. Schoultz believed rightly that the nobility must realize the necessity of reforms and carry them out before it was too late. His reforms were a small beginning and they aroused the wrath of his fellow noblemen, who denounced him as a traitor.

Schoultze's activities marked the beginning of an era of reform. Though his policy was not immediately imitated by men of his class, nevertheless the news of what he had done to improve the conditions of his serfs spread among the rural population in Estonia and Livonia. The Estonian and Latvian peasants began to wait for reforms which, they hopefully believed, would come sooner or later.

The work and ideas of the Estophils and Lettophils were of great importance in bringing about emancipation. The humanistic ideas of Eisen, Jannau, Hupel, Merkel and many other liberals from among the Germans disturbed the tranquility of the nobility in the Baltic provinces. This humanitarianism was a result in part of the French Revolutionary movement, which spread over Europe the liberal ideas of *Liberté, Egalité,* and *Fraternité.* Another circumstance which led some of the Estophils and Lettophils of Baltic feudalism to look for the wealth of national folklore, and thereby to question some of the assumptions of this class, was the Romantic Movement, with its revival of interest in the "people." Herder's writings on the folk cultures and national characters of the peoples of the world (including the Estonian) stimulated such an interest in the Baltic provinces, as elsewhere, and aroused in some persons a desire to preserve the Estonian folk culture which Hupel, Jannau, and other humanitarians had thought was dying. In their striving to preserve and collect the culture of the Estonians, the Estophils came to realize the inhuman conditions in which the Estonians lived. A complementary process also functioned. Through living among the people and becoming concerned with feudal conditions, some of the Estophils (Merkel, Hupel) grew interested in the culture of the common people. In either way the result was contempt for serfdom, love for the Estonian culture and an interest in preserving it—if not for the sake of its perpetuation, then at least to make it a museum piece. While realizing the brutality and injustice of serfdom, many, if not most, of the Estophils saw the wastefulness of this system. Their protest awakened an interest in improving the lot of the Estonians (or Latvians) on the part of the Russian government and even of some of the nobles themselves. The case of Baron Schoultz we have already noted. But the influence of the Estophils did not stop here. With their defense of the rights of the Estonian people to a more human existence, and with their interest in the preservation of Estonian folklore, they were the first to bring into the consciousness of the Estonians the importance of being an Estonian and the right to live as human beings, not as cattle. In such a way the first spark of Estonian national consciousness was kindled by the Estophils.

This was not done consciously, since the Estophils did not believe in the possibility of the Estonian peasant becoming a cultural nation. Most of them also did not forsee, nor did they propose, the immediate emancipation of the peasants. Aware of the backwardness of the Estonians, they believed that gradual emancipation would be more successful than immediate emancipation.

Whatever the limitations of humanitarianism and Estophilism, the century which produced the movements had laid the groundwork for far-reaching changes. In contrast to the dreary prospects at the end of the Great Northern War, the outlook for the Estonian nation at the opening of the nineteenth century was not without its gleams of promise.

3. The Beginning of Reforms: The 1804-06 Reforms of Alexander I and Their Impact Upon the Life of the Estonian Peasants

At the beginning of the nineteenth century the reformist ideas of Alexander I reached the Baltic provinces. At the same time the serf economy led the nobility themselves into economic crisis. Because of the luxurious life the nobles had been living, they reached the verge of bankruptcy. To save the barons from economic collapse, Alexander I agreed to

create for them a Bank of Credit *(Kreditkasse)* provided that
the barons would improve, through reforms, the living conditions of their peasants. The nobles believed that it would
be better to have the reforms carried through by their own
initiative rather than to be forced by the Czar. They, therefore, agreed to reforms—in Estonia (1802-04) and in Livonia
(1804). These reforms were practically the reinstatement of
the Swedish laws prior to the Northern War, but this time
the laws were less favorable to the peasants.[10]

Acordingly every Estonian peasant could become an owner
of land (therefore, this law was called *Igaüks*—which, in Estonian, means "everybody.") The selling and buying of peasants was limited and peasant courts were created in the
communities. For a better accountancy, books of payments,
that is, books showing how much the peasants owed their
landlord for the land they could call their own, were introduced.

There existed a difference between the reforms in Estonia
and Livonia. While in Estonia the nobles could expropriate
the peasants from their land quite easily, in Livonia they
could not. Also judicial rights of the nobility were greater in
Estonia than in Livonia. Even after all the reforms, the dues
charged the peasants were still above their ability to pay.
Control over the reforms was very weak and was, therefore,
almost completely ignored by the nobles. Practically, therefore, the economic conditions of the Estonian peasants did not
improve much despite the 1802-04 reforms in Livonia and
Estonia. The Estonian peasant continued to carry on his
miserable life as a serf until the beginning of the second
quarter of the nineteenth century.

4. Economic Conditions in the Cities During the Second
Half of the Eighteenth Century

As we have mentioned before, the cities in the Baltic
provinces were destroyed during the Great Northern War.

Only in the second half of the eighteenth century did the cities recover partly from the destruction. They were still ruled by medieval laws, such as those which enabled the guilds to dominate economic and political life of the city. The economic activities of the Estonian towns and cities were suited primarily to the internal market. Little export or import existed and no industry existed yet. The opening of the port of St. Petersburg sharply reduced the income from such cities as Tallinn (Reval), Pärnu (Pernau), and Narva, which lost their importance as ports. Nevertheless, contacts slowly developed during the second half of the eighteenth century with Germany, Holland, and England.[11] The importance of the inland towns was diminished also after the Great Northern War; Tartu (Dorpat), by losing its university, lost its cultural importance.

At the end of the eighteenth century new economic trends started to develop. The country began to recover slowly but steadily from the devastation of the war and the population began to increase. The nobles became interested in manufacturing as a new source of income. They began with the organization of small shops on their farms where they produced housewares and handicraft. With the increase of the demand for such products, the nobles began to organize small shops in the cities and, from those small beginnings, there later grew up factories. For example, a mirror factory, a watch factory, and a gun factory were constructed in Tallinn. The sheep-growing business was developing on the island of Dagö (Saaremaa); hence the industry of cloth production.[12] The establishment and growth of manufacturing was of great importance in fostering the general economic and cultural conditions in the Baltic provinces and with it the improvements of conditions for the Estonian peasants. It was also the beginning of the urbanization of the Estonian people— the seeds of the formation of an Estonian working and middle class.

5. Education and Religious Life During the Eighteenth Century

The Northern War destroyed the achievements of the educational reforms of the Swedes. The peasants who struggled for their existence barely had time for education. There were few teachers left after the Northern War, and those who became teachers did not have a good background. Only those men who were physically weak and unable to do other work became teachers. There were no buildings for public schools, and children were taught in stables and in the open air. Often the teacher had to go from farm to farm because of lack of facilities.

The 1730 law which required from the bride and groom reading abilities in order to get a marriage license, remained practically a dead letter. Under Catherine II the school question was raised again under Livonia's governor Browne, in 1765. He required that all children should be taught reading and writing. However, again because of lack of control, this requirement had no effect.[13] City schools were in as bad a condition as country schools. In addition to other poor educational facilities, there were but few schools for girls in Estonia and Livonia. Very slowly the educational facilities improved. New laws passed in 1750 required all Estonian parents to send their children to schools where religion, reading, and singing should be taught. Towards the end of the eighteenth century, however, education improved.

The clergyman's lack of knowledge of the Estonian language greatly diminished his influence. The German pastor was mainly dependent on the nobility and was regarded by the Estonians as such, that is, as an alien oppressor. The main purpose of the pastor was to teach the Estonian peasant obedience and respect to his master, the German noble. There did not exist personal contacts between the German pastor and the Estonian peasant. Relations were strictly official and businesslike, with no warmth from either side. Christianity

was regarded by the Estonian as something coming from the
nobles, and therefore a "must." The Sunday church visits
were regarded by the Estonian peasants as part of the feudal
obligations. It is, therefore, no wonder that, while nominally
Christians, the Estonian peasants still adhered to many pagan
customs during the eighteenth century.[14] The superior attitude of the German pastor to his oppressed Estonian parish-
ioner could not break those pagan habits. Christianity was
still a mere form and did not capture the innermost feelings
of the peasants.[15] A great change was brought into the religious life of the Estonians after the teachings of the Moravian
Brethren were introduced. In 1729 the first German preach-
ers from the Moravian church came into the Baltic provinces.
Their simple and democratic behavior found quick sympathy
among the Estonians. Instead of the deadly dogmatism of the
official Lutheran church, the Moravian Brethren approached
the Estonians with new emotional and religious inspiration.
The Lutheran church could hardly compete with the new
religious ideas and was losing more and more ground among
the Estonian population. Not only did the peasants become
enthusiastic followers of the Moravians: many nobles and
even some of the Lutheran clergy joined the new movement.[16] After the organizer of the Brethren, Zinzendorf,
visited Estonia and Livonia in 1732, the new religious revival
became a mass movement. This religious renaissance raised
the moral and spiritual level of the Estonian peasants. It resulted in a great reduction of alcoholism and thievery. It was
a positive factor in the rise of the cultural level of the Estonian people. With the success of the Moravian movement
among the Estonians, the nobles and the Lutheran church in
the Baltic provinces became more afraid of losing their power
and influence upon the native population.[17] The Moravian
Brethren, while increasing their strength, criticized more and
more the official system of serfdom, the low cultural level of
the peasants, and even the Lutheran church.

On behalf of the nobility and the Lutheran church the

new religious movement was forbidden by the Russian government in 1743. The Moravian churches were closed and their meetings were prohibited. But the Moravian movement could not be completely suppressed. For several decades it continued its existence among the Estonian peasants. In the long run, however, the new movement lost its mass character; and although it was again permitted by the Russian government in 1764, it never again reached its previous height.[18] Nonetheless, the Moravian movement had played a great role in forming the Estonian religious mind, in leading it towards a higher cultural level, and in transforming a lifeless, dogmatic Christianity into a living belief full of emotional inspirations and hopes.[19]

The Moravian movement had its part in promoting and fostering the development of the Estonian language by printing many books—among them the Bible—in the Estonian northern dialect of Tallinn, thus promoting this dialect to the position of a literary language, which ultimately became the literary language of the Estonian people. In this indirect way, the Moravians promoted Estonian cultural growth and, subsequently, the promotion of Estonian national consciousness.

The critical attitude of the Moravian Brethren towards the system of serfdom brought into the minds of the Estonian peasants their miserable life. The democratic attitude of the Brethren made the Estonian peasant feel like a human being, a feeling which he did not have prior to the arrival of the Moravians. Thus the Brethren were raising the suppressed social and national consciousness of the Estonians.

As mentioned before, the Brethren translated the Bible into the Estonian language; in future development the Bible became the cornerstone for Estonian literature.[20] After this beginning, many German books were translated into Estonian and in such a way brought enlightened ideas from Western Europe into the growing Estonian culture.

Nevertheless, despite these stirrings of the future, life in Estonia remained grim. While the eighteenth century was for Western Europe the philosophical century, bringing enlightenment into the European mind, and, while the French Revolution declared to mankind the rights of liberty, equality, and brotherhood, for the Estonian people, the eighteenth century and the beginning of the nineteenth century were still, on the whole, years of darkness, oppression, stagnation, and slavery.

Because the Estonian people had been separated politically from Western Europe and brought into the orbit of the Russian Empire and were under the complete economic, cultural, and religious control of the Baltic nobles, they lost their national consciousness for a long time. Only at the end of the eighteenth and the beginning of the nineteenth centuries did the ideas of the Age of Reason and of the French Revolution begin to penetrate the thick walls of German medieval serfdom and come into the Baltic provinces.

The rise of Estonian national consciousness during the following nineteenth century became possible because of the following factors:

1. The great change of the economic conditions from primitive serfdom into the rising capitalistic economy which forced the Baltic nobleman out of his estate into the competitive system of modern capitalism, where the peasants' productivity had to be increased through emancipation.

2. The enlightened ideas of German Idealism and those of the French Revolution, introduced by liberal-minded Germans such as Jannau, Eisen, Hupel, Merkel, and Schoultz, undermining the medieval society of the nobles.

3. The religious and moral revival of the Estonian people by the democratic teachings of the Moravian Brethren and the cultural revival brought about by translation of the Bible and the subsequent printing of Estonian books.

All these factors prepared the Estonians for the formation

and growth of national consciousness, which from the second half of the nineteenth century continued to grow among the more national-minded Estonian peasants, the growing middle class, and the emerging intellectuals.

CHAPTER II

Economic and Cultural Changes in Estonia during the Reign of Alexander I

1. Reforms of 1816-1819 and Attitude of the Baltic Nobles

In the previous chapter wc have seen how the Estonian peasants, economically ruined during the Great Northern War, slowly but persistently recuperated during the second half of the eighteenth century.[1] During the first quarter of the nineteenth century the Estonians went through the experience of intense religious revival;[2] they also became an object of interest and sympathy by German humanitarians,[3] and they began the new century with their gradual emancipation, given them by Alexander I.

This made the Estonian people more and more aware of their servile position. As a result of expanded educational facilities, to be discussed presently, the number of peasants who could read and write grew steadily. Owing in part to the better schooling, and in part to the disappointment with the reforms of 1802-4, the apathetic attitude, which had been so strong among the Estonian people since the last vestiges of resistance and consciousness were destroyed during the early Middle Ages, began to vanish. It gave place to a growing desire on the part of the peasants to be treated more humanly as well as to become sole owners of the land they had been tilling for centuries.[4]

29

This desire for economic independence was, as we mentioned before, greatly facilitated by educational growth during the second half of the nineteenth century. As compared with Russia and even with parts of Western Europe, the Estonian countryside came to enjoy a somewhat advanced school system provided by the German landlords. Actually, formal schools were organized by the Teutonic Knights as early as 1692.[5] Those were small church schools, where peasant children were taught reading, writing and the catechism. The number of church schools decreased during and after the Great Northern war; after the recuperation of the country, however, they spread more and more widely over Estonia and Livonia. By 1788 most of the Lutheran churches had schools and there were few Estonian children between the ages of seven and nine who did not read and write.[6] The actual, though not official, purpose of those schools was to develop among the Estonian peasants the attitude of servility and humility toward their masters, the Baltic nobles. The curriculum was meager, the physical plant poor, and the quality of teaching low.

During the Napoleonic wars economic conditions in Estonia deteriorated greatly, since the Russian government heavily taxed the Baltic provinces,[7] and Napoleon's Continental blockade was ruinous. Only after Napoleon's collapse could Alexander I finally achieve what he wanted from the Baltic nobles and what he failed to achieve during the 1804 reform: the complete emancipation of the peasants.

In 1811 the Estonian Diet passed the Emancipation Bill and Alexander signed it in 1816. The Livonian Diet followed with a similar bill in 1818 and the Tsar signed it in 1819, These laws seemed to be a great victory for the few liberals among the nobles, who had seen the dream of Merkel and Jannau and all the other German humanitarians come true.

Actually, the emancipation worsened the economic conditions of the peasants and made them even more helpless prey to their former landlords.[8] According to the new laws the

Estonian peasant became a free man: he could no longer be bought or sold by his landlord. Nor could his landlord force him to work. But at the same time he lost his right of tenant-ship over the land he was tilling, and thence forth he could be evicted from the farm he was working, where his fore-fathers had worked for centuries. The new law also freed the landlord from his responsibility to feed the peasant in times of stress. The same law reserved for the landlord his right of determining the rent the peasant had to pay him for the use of the land. This so-called emancipation turned the Estonian peasant from a serf into a landless proletarian whose rights, so high-sounding in the Bill, became actually a whip in the hands of the Baltic noble—still, in effect, his master.[9]

The great disappointment of the Estonian peasants after the Emancipation was enacted can, therefore, be easily under-stood.[10] We know of many cases where peasants refused to accept their freedom.[11] At the beginning, the nobles, too, viewed emancipation with fear and suspicion. By nature, traditionally conservative, they were afraid of any change. They agreed with the emancipation proposals of Alexander I only half-heartedly, and, as we have mentioned before, under the pressure of economic circumstances. But their worries and suspicions soon disappeared after they found out that they had gained more actual power over the peasants by giv-ing them nominal rights of freedom. Now they could force their former tenants to work as hard as they wished them to, since they could evict them when the latter could not pay rent. Since the Baltic nobles were becoming familiar with many new luxuries, travelling more and more extensively abroad, and often visiting the Tsar's court in St. Petersburg, they were looking for new ways and means to increase their income from their peasants.[11]

How did the nobility look upon their former serfs? There was little change of heart about the qualities of the peasant, as we can see from contemporary German writers,[12] who make it clear that the Baltic nobles both feared and despised the Estonians. As in comparison with the neighbors of the Estonians, the Latvians, the nobles considered the Estonians much more stubborn and proud than the Latvians, whom they subjugated and controlled more easily.

This we can confirm from historical evidence, which tells us that the Latvians' resistance towards the Teutonic Knights was much less than that of their Estonian neighbors. Even afterwards, the Latvians adjusted themselves to their masters more rapidly, while the Estonians continued to rebel violently. As a German contemporary observed, the Baltic nobles still considered the Estonians with suspicion. Since the latter valued freedom above everything and, the Baltic nobles were convinced, would seize the very first opportunity to revolt against their masters. The Germans in Tartu still judged the Estonian national character more highly than that of the Latvians, whom they despised as weaklings and cowards while they feared the Estonians.[13]

2. Living Conditions of the Estonian Peasants after 1819

What were the conditions in which the Estonians lived after their emancipation? Again we have to resort to contemporary evidence.

The Estonian peasant-household, writes the observant German traveller, J. G. Kohl:

... is the extreme of poverty, filth, disorder and need, and there is nothing similar in the whole of Europe . . . Their food is extremely miserable, and there is no doubt that some tribesman in their wigwams had more comfort than could be found in an Estonian household [literally: apartment].[14]

During the winter the living-room is also a place for chickens; the benches, tables and chairs of the Estonians look as if they had grown in the forest . . . and it is obvious that, from the outstanding progress and improvement which the rest of Europe achieved in the arts and crafts, not a particle has reached this people, which still remains in the same prehistoric condition as its ancestors were in since time immemorial.[15]

Lights and candles they do not know. The aspect of those Estonian villages is the saddest in the world. The houses stand crooked, the roofs covered or uncovered, half of them rotten . . . most houses are inhabited, but many are deserted, because the peasants had moved and settled [in different places]. There is barely a trace of gardening.[16]

Little was done by the landlord, especially after the emancipation, to help the peasant improve his lot, since he was now a free man. In addition to this misery, there came another source of poverty: alcoholism. This was not a new escape mechanism to the Estonian peasant, who through the centuries of oppression had tried to forget his troubles by drinking. But during the 1820's and later drunkenness was greatly facilitated by an ingenious idea of the nobles for increasing their income by distilling alcohol from potatoes, which were recently introduced and were grown in abundance. Distilled spirits became one of the best sources of income for noblemen, and the Estonian peasant became a splendid customer, forced to cultivate potatoes and to spend more of his income than he should on alcohol. Kohl describes the alcoholism of the Estonian peasant thus:

The greed of the [Estonian] people for this poisoned "water of repentance" is above any concept . . . The landlords, especially in Estonia, receive their greatest revenue from the distilleries and from the inns.[17] Therefore the landlords do nothing against such a bad habit, and they even encourage it, as can be seen from the fact, that temperance societies, which began to spread here, were forbidden.[18]

Such an attitude on the part of the nobles, as witnessed by Kohl, a German, and by many others who had the opportunity to be in Estonia during the first half of the nineteenth century, could hardly promote the economic and cultural growth of the Estonian peasants, but rather tended to perpetuate the centuries-long enslavement, though disguised by formal freedom.

Under such conditions, under which the peasants had to work for the landlords as hard as ever, without the slightest hope of becoming landowners and with no rise in living standards, to provide them with education, no national consciousness could ever develop among them.[19]

The Estonian peasants did not call themselves a nation but *Maarahvas,* that is, country-folk. An Estonian people with representatives of all classes, or at least two, as in other feudal and oriental states, did not exist. The more than six hundred years of enslavement destroyed any national feeling the people had, and paralyzed the Estonian peasant into a trance which, according to the will and intentions of the masters, the Baltic nobles, should have lasted eternally. How remote any national consciousness was from the mind of the Estonians during those years we can see on the example of those peasants, who, settling in the cities, tried to become good Germans, adopting the German language and customs, trying to merge with the lower-class Germans. They would feel hurt and humiliated if their less fortunate brethren would still consider them as Estonians.[20]

As a matter of fact, those *Kadakasksad,** as they were called by the peasants in the villages, did not want to be called peasants any more, but began to feel like city-folk. The reason was that "peasant" and "Estonian" were then synonymous. The desire of every ambitious and free Estonian peasant who had the opportunity to go to the city was to break forever with his past, with his belonging to the despised, filthy, uneducated peasant mass, and to identify himself with the class of his master—the German.[21]

3. Beginnings of Urbanization

Since in the village the Estonian always felt the overlordship of his baron, his natural desire was to escape from it. The only possibility of doing so was to migrate into the cities and towns. The peasant knew the city from previous experiences, while visiting it occasionally, and admired the city-dweller's independence of the nobleman. By observation, the peasant realized the privileged position of the townspeople as in contrast to his own dependence upon the absolute will of the nobleman. In addition to this independence, the Estonian peasant envied the city people their freedom from being subject to enlistment into the army; (since the towns did not have to provide for soldiers, but instead had to pay taxes).[22]

Recruitment was one of the hardest burdens of the Estonian peasants. According to Russian Imperial law, every county had to provide a certain number of soldiers. Usually the poorest had to go, since the wealthy could pay in order to avoid service. If the community could not provide an adult male, a child was then taken, and sent to the military school in Reval (Tallinn).[23]

This recruitment system was the most horrible in all of Europe. It consisted of serving in the Russian army for twenty-five consecutive years. Most Estonians taken into the army rarely returned. And those who did, after twenty-five years of living among Russians and speaking Russian, could hardly speak a word of Estonian. Seldom would they know anyone in their native village. In addition to this, at the very beginning of their service the Estonian recruits were forced into the Russian Orthodox Church.[24] This factor alone would be sufficient to stimulate a strong movement of the peasants into the cities and towns. It obviously could not be done prior to the peasant's emancipation, since he was tied to the land. But after 1818 many tried to go to the cities. It was not easy, however, for a peasant to break with his farm.

During the 1820's and 1830's the cities were small, and especially after the emergence of St. Petersburg and Riga as commercial ports, the towns of Tallinn, Pärnu and Narva lost their economic importance as ports.[25] The local German middle and lower classes could maintain themselves and did not need any help. Also the nobles lived mostly on their estates and only went to the cities during the winter months, for entertainment, and once every three years for election of their representatives to the Diet and other local *Ritterschaften*. Therefore, there was little hope for a peasant to settle in a town unaided. Strict medieval guild-laws were still in force and were another handicap for the peasants who desired to enter the many crafts.

The guilds in the cities, owing to their privileges, were in a much better position than the peasants, even after the emancipation of the latter. Therefore, we can understand the peasants' desire to move into the cities and to be freed from their obligations to state, landlord, and clergy. The growth of the cities was retarded by the economic depression in the country which began on the eve and lasted until after the middle of the nineteenth century.[26] The economic crisis was a result of the changing economy of the world, the transition from feudalism into capitalism and the growing dependency of the Estonian landlord-economy, formerly self-sufficient, upon the world market.[27] The economic crisis was also partly due to the nobles' experimental changes in agriculture, the introduction of mixed farming, and the lack of understanding on the part of the uneducated peasants, as well as lack of willingness to work hard enough for their landlords and for themselves. Since the peasant was no longer certain of having the same land for more than the renting period, he was interested only in exploiting the land, a usage which resulted in land-exhaustion and famine.[28]

Very slowly the growing cities established new economic enterprises—the factory and shop. First in the cities like Tallinn and Pärnu, then in Tartu and Narva, textile factories were created, and the need for workers increased. However, bad roads greatly hampered the economic interchange between city and country for a long time.[29]

The growth of Tartu was greatly facilitated by the refounding of its university in 1802. Tartu again became the cultural center of the Baltic provinces. With the years, it

developed into one of the most outstanding liberal universities of the Russian empire; its fame spread all over Europe
and attracted many students from abroad, especially from
Germany.[30]

All this stimulated the flow of peasants into the cities. But
it was a very slow process, and until the third quarter of the
nineteenth century the cities remained what they had been
for centuries: the bastions of Germandom, where the first
centers of the Estonian population were beginning to form.

4. Beginnings of Germanization

The economic and legal emancipation of the peasants at
the beginning of the nineteenth century was followed by a
cultural emancipation tending toward Germanization. This
was the result of many factors. First of all, the educational
system itself did not provide for higher education in the
Estonian language. Only elementary schools gave the peasant
children some knowledge in their native Estonian tongue.
This was actually the aim of those Germans who had some
thoughts about the future of the Estonian people. None of
the so-called liberals thought of any cultural emancipation
of the Estonians within their own language. Literacy in the
mother tongue was to be used only as the first step towards
Germanization. It was clear to every thinking peasant that, in
order to advance in the social scale, he would have to em-
brace the German culture. Mastery of the German language
was the basic criterion for education. The moment a peasant
left the village, he tried to assimilate the German culture,
that is, the German language. It was natural that the Estonian
language was used only among peasants. Every one in a position superior to the peasant—the foreman, the distiller, the
brewer, the supervisor, the cobbler, and even members of the
clergy, whether of German or Estonian descent—used German as his language. At the beginning men of such occupa-
tions came from Germany, but, with the years, Estonians

entered those fields. Thus Estonians had to converse with their superiors in German; and after moving to the cities, they continued to use German within their families.[31]

In the cities the Estonian former peasant dealt with the German craftsmen and merchants, his superiors. The road towards Germanization was free, and many went smoothly ahead toward complete assimilation. The aim of the Baltic German, on the other hand, was not directed toward assimilation of the Estonian peasant. This can be seen from the little effort they put forth in educating the Estonians. There were still no good teachers during the 1830's and 1840's. Only those peasants who were not fit for physical work became teachers. The quality of teaching was therefore very low. There was one method of training: a child had to learn the alphabet, not in a systematic way, but by learning excerpts from the catechism and memorizing them.[32]

The children had to repeat sentences after the teacher, until they had memorized them. They rarely knew what they read. Despite this method, the children were taught the minimum of reading and writing. Because of their poverty, few among the peasant children could dream of continuing their education. Here we can observe a very interesting phenomenon among the Germans during those years: the general attitude towards the Estonians was that of sympathy (by the more human and liberal), contempt (by the majority of the Balts), or, in many instances, lack of interest. No German, were he as humanistic and liberal as Merkel or Jannau, ever thought of the emancipation of the Estonian peasants in terms of the renaissance of Estonian culture.[33] What the Estophils envisaged for the Estonian people was their emancipation from the primitiveness of Estonian culture, which was, according to their beliefs, destined to go into museums. The Estonian people would become part of the German people, and thus fulfilling the old dream of the Teutonic Knights: the complete Germanization of the Baltic provinces. Those were the views, though not always openly expressed, but in their inner-

most heart cherished by the liberal-minded who believed
that assimilation of the Estonian peasant would lead him
toward complete freedom. They could think of nothing else
owing to their own education and beliefs, which led them to
regard German culture as superior to others.[34]

Most Baltic Germans, however, were mainly concerned
with the Estonian peasants' ability to take care of the land.
They were less concerned with the spiritual or educational
development and life of the peasant mass. Nevertheless, the
little education the Estonians received was steadily, though
slowly, lending them towards denationalization. In this process the Lutheran church and its clergy took an active part. In
this concern Kohl observed in his book on the Baltic provinces:

One of the most noticeable phenomena is the denationalization
of these nations [Estonians] and their. . . . transformation into
Germans. As uneducated slaves they rigidly kept through the
centuries their paternal habits, their old poetry, their national
clothing, their pagan superstitions and their barbaric ignorance.[35]

Kohl and many other liberal Germans therefore believed
that, through education in the basic elements of German
culture, which would come to them through their German
masters, the Estonians would tend more and more towards
adopting German culture. Kohl believed it was too late, even
if there were any sense in doing so, to elevate the Estonian
language into the sphere of cultural languages, and thus
create an advanced, specifically Estonian, culture, since the
educated Estonians resented being called Estonians or being
dragged back to their nationality.[36] Since those few Estonians
who were free and educated showed such a tendency, it is no
wonder that such a sharp observer and critic of the miserable
conditions of the Estonian people as Kohl had to come to
such a conclusion.

Even the process of Germanization, however, as seen by

the liberals, was a far-off dream because of the slow rate with which this process would go on, and because of the prevailing conditions in the Baltic provinces during this period. Despite the reforms of Alexander I in 1804, in 1816, and in 1819, the power of the Baltic nobility was not appreciably diminished. Not only were the nobles firmly in power in the three Baltic provinces; their influence was felt in St. Petersburg and many other parts of Russia. Since the times of Peter the Great, the German nobility in the Baltic provinces had made a name as the most faithful servants of the Russian Tsars. Many Baltic nobles held influential positions at court at St. Petersburg.[37] In the Baltic provinces they managed to cling to some important vestiges of their feudal system despite the fact that all over Europe feudalism was being crushed by the French Revolution. The Baltic nobility continued to rule the country, almost monopolizing the provincial diets, being free from taxes and recruitment, and retaining great actual power over the peasantry, and maintaining their feudal relationship to their less noble German burghers and clergy as they had done before.[38] The Baltic provinces remained an historical anachronism in a Europe which had seen the feudal order destroyed. The majority of the noblemen realized that the Estonian peasant could not be kept in slavery, as had been done for centuries. Nevertheless, there still were many who dreamed about the good old days when the peasant was in complete dependence upon his master. Such an attitude was openly expressed by Baron Freiherr von Ungern-Sternberg, who wrote that the peasant, together with the farm and inventory, belonged to the landlord and his heirs. The landlord had absolute command of the peasant's services, whether it was common labor or any talent the peasant possessed in arts and crafts.[39]

CHAPTER III

The Failure of Liberalism and the End of the
Manorial System

1. Agricultural Conditions and Conversion

However illusory the freedom obtained by the Estonian peasants through the emancipation laws of 1816 and 1819, they did acquire the rights of a limited self-government, restricted to participation in their community council and in the peasant courts. This became a step towards their maturity and an educational factor which greatly fostered their self confidence. However little they had to say or decide— and the landlords knew how to control completely even this little independence—this small share of self-government had a very strong influence on the development of the peasants' mental ability to think for themselves, and increased their self-respect—a development symbolized also by the adoption of family names, which the peasants did not have prior to emancipation.[1]

The reforms came, as mentioned before, mainly because the landlords themselves could not meet expenses with the income from their estates. By giving the peasants nominal freedom, they got the opportunity to increase the latter's obligations and thus to experiment with new crops. The major change was the change from a three-field system to a many-crop system, where the crops were changed systematically, in order to limit the exploitation of the soil.[2] This was a result from the economic crisis in the Baltic provinces due to the tremendous crash of the prices on grain, which, in its turn was a result of the collapse of world-market prices, on which the Baltic provinces were greatly dependent.

The new agricultural policy of the landlords consisted of the introduction of wool-raising and the development of a strong dairy-economy. Potatoes and fodder crops too, became more important. This radical change in agricultural methods became an additional burden to the peasant, whose work increased while his income did not. The intensive agricultural system also brought the piece-work system of payment into use, and thereby put another whip into the hands of the landlord. In addition to the maladjustments of these years of experimentation, the Baltic provinces were plagued with droughts. Altogether the position of the peasant deteriorated steadily. Hunger and starvation became common, since the landlord no longer had to care for his free peasant. As a result of all these changes, tremendous dissatisfaction grew among the peasant mass.

In their misery the peasants accused the nobles. They believed that the latter were cheating them of their rights given through the emancipation. They considered the Tsar as misinformed about the noblemen's chicanery. Somehow rumors spread through the countryside during the late 1830's that the Russian government was giving land to all those peasants who would apply to be put on a "list" for getting land in Russia. Growing numbers of Estonian peasants went to Riga, then the administrative center of the Russian governor and of the Russian Orthodox Church. Despite the public insistence of the Russian and German officials to the contrary, the rumors spread more and more, and the flow of peasants increased steadily.[3]

The police could not chase them away from Riga. The peasants went to the Russian clergy, there asking for help against the German noblemen, since they knew about the

growing rivalry between the Lutheran and the Russian Orthodox churches and hoped to benefit from it. The Russian
Church authorities made the mistake of taking the names of
the peasants, which increased even more among the latter
their conviction in the truthfulness of the rumors of aid of
Russian government and church against their German oppressors. Things went too far, however, even for the Russians,
who, at the beginning, looked with pleasure upon the mounting troubles of the German nobility. Many nobles whose
peasants left the estates complained to the court in St. Petersburg, and orders came from the Tsar to stop this nonsense.
It was not so easy, however, to send the distressed peasants
home. The Russian government had to use force, and many
a bloody fight developed between the Russian army and
police on one side, and the angered and desperate Estonians
on the other. All this ended very tragically for the peasants.
Hundreds were arrested, many killed, many tried and sent
to Siberia, many beaten and given later to the army.

Nevertheless, this frightful experience did not change the
belief of the peasants in the ultimate help of the Russian government and the Russian Orthodox Church. New rumors
spread and increased. This time the peasants grasped for their
last help: the Russian Orthodox Church. They believed that
by becoming Greek Orthodox they would receive land in
Russia proper and become free landowners. This movement
began again in the Latvian part of Livonia, where the Russian Bishop Philaret sought to undermine the Lutheran
church by accepting Latvian peasants into the Orthodox
church. Thousands of Estonian peasants again flooded Riga,
and this time they were received with open arms by the
Russian clergy and taken into the Russian church.[4] The
Lutheran Church tried in every way to retaliate by preaching
the sinfulness of trading the old belief for a new, and by dis-
puting the hopes of the Estonian peasants of getting land
after being confirmed into the new church. Nothing, however, could stop the peasants from deserting the Lutheran

Church. They wanted so much to escape from their present hopeless conditions that the pastors' words did not appeal to them at all.

This movement of thousands of Estonian peasants into the Russian Orthodox Church died out by itself after 1848. The reason was that after the converted peasants returned home nothing changed for the better in their life. The economic improvement, the land which they hoped to receive in Russia, did not come about. By that time tens of thousands of Estonians, mainly from the Southern provinces of Tartumaa, Virumaa and Valgamaa, had embraced the Orthodox faith.[5] This resulted in a division among the Estonian people into Lutheran and Russian Orthodox communities. It was an unnecessary burden which the traditionally Lutheran Estonians had taken on themselves out of despair. This movement, which began in the 1840's and lasted for almost a decade, brought only misery to the life of the peasants. It was made possible by their extreme exploitation by the German nobles, by the hopelessness of the peasants, and by their lack of confidence in the Lutheran Church and its clergy.

The beatings, trails, and persecution taught the Estonian peasants a very hard lesson: that neither the German landlords nor the Russian government was his friend. The first truth the Estonian peasants knew from the experience of six centuries. The second they learned during the upheaval of the 1840's.

The obvious failure of the reforms of 1816 and 1819, which resulted in much hardship to the peasants and in confusion and trouble for the Russian government during the 1840's, indicated to the Russian government and to the new Tsar, Nicholas, I, the necessity of further reform in the Baltic provinces.[6]

During the 1820's and 1830's, despite the economically desperate conditions of the peasants, the German Baltic nobility enjoyed to the fullest degree the privileges of their position; they did not seem to worry about the shortcoming of the emancipation of the peasants after 1816 and 1819. Few among the nobles gave thought to the idea of radical improvement of the lot of their tenants and laborers. The nobles regarded their privileges, economic as well as political, as something eternal and beyond criticism. Nevertheless the ideas of peasant emancipation in Western Europe (particularly in Prussia) and the ideas of the French Revolution and of German humanism found some support among the more liberal and enlightened Baltic nobles.

2. The Liberal Decades (1820-1849) and the Following Unrest

During the period 1820-1849, there was formed among the nobles a liberal group which found the support of the Russian government. The most outstanding men among this group were Hamilkar von Fölkersahm (1811-1856) and Samson von Himmelstierna (1778-1858).[7] Fölkersahm and Samson were both leading figures in the so-called radical-liberal wing of the nobility, a group dissatisfied with the 1816 and 1819 reforms. Thanks to the activities of this group, particularly to Fölkersahm, a new agricultural reform was inaugurated in 1849.[8] It greatly improved the lot of the peasants, narrowing the power of the landlords, and giving to the peasant community for use land which the nobles could never expropriate. The measure also introduced the monetary rent, which, the liberal nobles believed, should substitute the oppressive system of forced labor.[9]

Unfortunately for the development of the country, the liberals soon lost their strong influence, and the conservatives again took a lead in affairs. The new reforms did not have much time to get started; conditions among the peasants did not improve during the late forties and early fifties.[10] Many of the liberal nobles lost their courage after the mass conversion and the many outbreaks of violence among the peasants. Lack of knowledge among the peasants in follow-

ing the innovations the nobles had introduced brought a
steady increase of hunger and despair among the Estonian
population.

All this served to increase the tension between the nobles
and the peasants, especially after the 1849 reforms.[11] The
peasants believed that the nobles did not have any right to
force them to work and that the nobles were wilfully hiding
their rights from them. In many places peasants refused to
work because of this feeling. In parts of Estonia and Northern Livonia small revolts occurred, in which the peasants
tried force, but were crushed by police and soldiers. Such
explosions of peasant hatred usually ended in death for many,
and public beating and expulsion into Siberia for the remainder. The bloodiest of all such revolts were in the estate
of Mahtra, in 1858, and in Harju.[12] Both were suppressed,
and hundreds of peasants were sent to Siberia; public flog-
gings and the hanging of nine peasants was the culmination.

These uprisings were not organized or planned. They came
about spontaneously and without any known leadership.
There was no Estonian middle class or intelligentsia to incite
the peasants to rebel against their oppressors. It was the
wretched condition of rural life that brought about such outbursts of despair.[13]

3. Education and Religious Life During the Period
1820-1860

Despite economic stagnation and, in many respects, deteri-
oration during the thirties and forties, educational facilities
spread slowly. In connection with the emancipation of
1816-19 the government put forward a law concerning education among the peasants which required for each village
or community a school which children from the age of ten
must attend until they should receive from the pastor certifi-
cates indicating their satisfactory ability to read and write
and a knowledge of the catechism.[14] They were also to learn

how to sing church songs; the school term was to be from
November 10 until March 10. In addition every parish with
a population of 2000 had to have a parish school where at
least twelve male students should obtain their education. The
latter would after graduation, be obliged to work as secre-
taries or teachers in a given community.[14]

The parish schools were a step forward in the cultural
emancipation of the Estonian peasants. In those parish
schools the pupils were taught for five days a week. Both the
pupils and the teacher lived in the school. During the week-
end the pupils went home. The curriculum of the schools
consisted of Biblical history, Catechism, religious songs, writing, reading, and arithmetic. All such schools were super-
vised by the pastors. Curiously enough, the result of this system of teaching was that the pupils were very familiar with
the history of the Jews, but not at all with that of the Russian Tsars!

With the inauguration of the parish schools and the mul-
tiplication of schools in the villages, there arose the need for
more teachers. For the training of new teachers a teacher
seminary, supported by the provincial diets was founded in
Valga by the Bishop Ferdinand Walter.[15] The language of
instruction was German.

This seminary was led for a long time by a liberal-minded
Latvian, Johannes Zimse (1814-1881), a teacher by profession
and education. Zimse himself received a German education,
but was very liberal and sympathetic towards the national
awakening among the Latvians and Estonians. His influence
was of primary importance in strengthening the self-respect
of the young teachers and in fostering love towards the teaching profession, as well as in developing in the students the
ability to think for themselves and the desire to further their
education and widen their cultural horizons.[16] Zimse was
thus responsible for laying the foundations of a new Estonian
generation, which, having obtained the tools of education
through the German school, became interested in spreading

and raising the standard of Estonian culture among the peasants. Of Zimse's more than 400 pupils, about 100 were Estonians. From among them emerged teachers, musicians, and political activists—the advance guard of the renaissance of Estonian national consciousness.

In addition to the seminary in Valga, a second seminary for the preparation of elementary school teachers was created in Tartu and was led successfully by a German religious educator, Friedrich August Wilhelm Hollmann (1833-1900). Hollmann was not sympathetic towards the national aspirations of the Estonian and Latvian peoples; his aim was the preservation of the German Baltic tradition and political system.[17] He could not, however, entirely suppress the growing desire of the Estonian and Latvian students to remain Estonian or Latvian.

Many graduates from the Tartu seminary went into elementary schools within the city, where German was the only language of instruction despite the fact that the majority of students attending those schools during the fifties and sixties were from among the urbanized peasants—craftsmen, workers, servants, etc. There were no schools in the towns with Estonian as the language of instruction. Only the villages—community and parish schools in the villages—used Estonian as the language of instruction. This lack of Estonian instruction in the town schools was a hindering factor in the creation of an urban Estonian middle class. The prevailing assumption among the nobles and burghers was that in the cities the Estonian population would tend towards assimilation.

4. The *Köster* as the Bearer of Culture in the Village

If the teachers' seminaries gave impetus to the awakening of the Estonian national consciousness, of no less importance for the preservation of the Estonian language was the folk-poetry and customs—the work of the Estonian *köster* (sexton), the assistant to the German pastor in the community. Neither the pastor nor his assistant received a salary. For their income they received land, sometimes of considerable size for the pastor, but of lesser proportions for the sextons. Significantly, the peasants called the pastor "church lord" *(kirikuhärra)*.[18]

The tilling of the lands of the pastors and sexton was the obligation of the peasants, who also had to supply the clergyman with products from their households, such as meat, poultry, wood, and wool. It very often happened that the pastor had to collect his dues from the peasants with the aid of the courts: the peasants did not consider him as their spiritual superior, but as their second landlord. The pastor, being an educated man among an ignorant people, with little or no knowledge of the native language, very often full of prejudices against the Estonians, showed little love or understanding towards his community. In return he met with aloofness and hatred, concealed in most cases behind forced reverence. Most of the time the pastor fulfilled his duties as he was obliged to do, without showing much warmth toward the community which he was serving, and whose food and labor he was using. The German pastor and the Estonian peasant were of two distinct worlds, without mutual trust or respect.[19] It was natural that emotionally the pastor could never understand the peasant, unless he really went out of his superior atmosphere and tried to follow Estonian patterns of thinking. Few pastors, however, did this; the main purpose of the majority was to mediate the landlord and the peasant in matters of soul and conscience.

The work the pastor fulfilled was of routine character: on Sundays the peasants were called for group baptisms, marriages and funerals, all done after the Sunday-services.

The peasants regularly attended the church, but it was done in a matter-of-fact fashion, without soul or heart. Therefore, the pastor had little influence upon the peasants. The peasants in their turn called the church obligations

Kirikuorjus, that is church-slavery, a term which expressed
their whole attitude toward the pastor and the church. Thus
pagan habits could still be found, even as late as the second
half of the nineteenth century. Pagan superstitions were also
flourishing. If there were any Christian beliefs and morals
among the peasants, the Estonian *köster* was responsible.
He came from among the peasants, knew their life and their
thoughts, lived in poverty similar to the peasants', spoke the
same language, and showed warmth and understanding towards them in their work and life. The peasants loved him
and respected him, as can be seen from the fact that the *köster*
had his land tilled by the peasants with diligence and love,
without any pressure.[20]

The cultural life in the village was carried on patiently
by the Estonian teachers. Theirs was a life of daily hardships, struggling with poverty themselves, often teaching in
barns in the fields; during the cold winter months they
walked for miles from house to house teaching the three R's
to peasant children who could not travel for lack of winter
clothing. Since many teachers joined the Moravian movement, the meetings of the members were held in the school
buildings. The village schoolteachers performed the partly
religious function of leading the well-attended meetings.

Thus the *kösters,* the schoolteachers, and the very dutiful
German and Estonian pastors were responsible for giving
moral support to the Estonian population, keeping the few
sparks of Christianity alive among the peasants, and spreading among them enough education to keep the Estonian
spirit alive during dark times of slavery and the scarcely
lighter times of manorial labor.

5. The Outlook on Mid-Century

The disappointing outcome of the agrarian laws of 1816-19
was due to the manorial labor which followed. During the
1830's and 1840's, this manorial labor system greatly ham-

pered the development of a stronger peasant economy which had been the original intention of the liberal nobles. Though the Estonian peasant could leave his community, the rigid guild laws in the cities stopped him from entering the crafts. During the forties, a limited number of peasants preferred working as servants in the cities, or at any kind of urban labor, to working for the landlords in the village. During those years, many landlords proposed limiting the peasants' rights to leave their communities. This they proposed in order to assure the existence of the village community. Such a movement was in contradiction of the emancipation so strongly proclaimed by the Livonian Diet. In order to stimulate the peasant to work harder and improve his land, liberal-minded landlords proposed abolishing the manorial system and substituting for it monetary rents. This idea did not find immediate support among the landlords, who feared losing their grip upon the peasants. It also did not find immediate support among the peasants, since the latter, used to centuries-old manorial labor, saw in every new order another trick by the landlords to keep them in bondage. After Baron Theodor Hahn-Postenden first introduced monetary rent on his Courland estate in 1839, squires in all of the Baltic provinces followed, slowly but steadily.

It took more than twenty years (1847-1868) to change from the manorial to the rental system in Estonian and Northern Livonia. During this time conditions in the Estonian provinces changed very much. The great majority of peasants did not own their land, but rented it. Those of them who paid in money obtained it by cultivating flax, which impoverished their soil. Since they did not own the land, they cared nothing about its preservation. Although they cultivated sixteen times more land than the German landlords, they produced only twice the amount of major products, a fact which indicates the low standard of their life and agricultural tools.[21]

Before 1848 most peasants lived in compact farm villages. During the first twenty years of the rental system the picture changed: the villages were supplanted by individual farms, where the farmhouse occupied the center, with all the farmlands surrounding it. Such a development fostered more personal interest among the peasants in improving their farms and increasing their wealth, and an ambition constantly to improve farmland and agricultural techniques.[22]

At the time when the village was beginning to improve owing to the ultimate success of the rental system, the development of the cities and towns lagged behind. The main cause for the faster development of the village was the 1849 reform. The slowness of the cities and towns was caused by the rigid laws of the guilds and the strict regimentation of craftsmanship.[23]

Until the 1840's there were so many limitations to the development of the crafts that they could never outgrow their narrow, medieval forms. The master of each craft was restricted in the number of his apprentices; he was assigned a special place for selling; often even the amount of production was controlled. Such limitations did not allow for the development of free competition, the basis of increased production and the beginning of mass production and the factory system. Thus the ex-peasant, though nominally free, could not enter the guilds. There was no room for Estonian competition with the German craftsman.

During those years of transition there arose the question of giving to the peasants the church lands, which the pastor usually owned, and which he lived on. Some liberal churchmen believed that it would be of great help to the peasants to rent them some of their land. More liberal pastors even played with the idea of leasing the land for life, so that the peasant would be more interested in putting all his energy into the land. They considered asking from the peasants only 10 per cent of the value of the land; the rest of the debt would rest indefinitely on the land, thus making the peasant an eternal renter. A still more liberal group argued that the land should be sold to the peasants in full ownership in order to develop in them more interest in working and improving it. This discussion continued for some time in the liberal periodical *Baltische Monatschrift,* but such proposals, if ever realized, were never carried out on a large scale.[24]

How did the Baltic nobles look upon the emancipation of the Estonian peasants under the rental system? Most of them accepted emancipation as a necessary evil, and, with the exception of a more liberal minority, the nobility looked upon the rental system as sufficient reform for future generations.[25]

CHAPTER IV

The Beginnings of National Awakening

1. The Estonian Learned Society and its Predecessors

There is no certain date or particular event which can be designated as the beginning of Estonian national consciousness. The emerging process of national consciousness was a long one, due to many factors which had begun at the time of the Estophils. Thus the revival of Estonian language and folk culture was of primary importance for the revival of Estonia as a nation. It was at the beginning of the nineteenth century that interest in the Estonian language among the German clergy produced considerable results.

Pastor Johann Heinrich Rosenplänter (1782-1846) was the center of a group of such men interested in the Estonian language. Both a teacher and a pastor by profession, he early showed great interest in the language. Around him Rosenplänter gathered several enthusiastic Estophils: Peter Heinrich von Frey (1757-1833), Johann Wilhelm Ludwig von Luce (1750-1842), Arnold Friedrich Johann Knüpffer (1777-1843), Otto Reinhold von Holz (1751-1828), and Otto Wilhelm Masing (1763-1832), the last-named being of Estonian and Swedish origin.[1] Rosenplänter was greatly influenced by the liberal ideas spread over Europe after the French Revolution. As the result of his research, he published in Pärnu between 1813 and 1832, in twenty volumes, a most fundamental work on the Estonian language, *Beiträge zur genau-ern Kenntniss der ehstnischen Sprache*. This monumental work represented a great personal financial cost to its author, since such a voluminous publication, of only a limited interest to the European public, could not become a financial success. With this work Rosenplänter greatly helped his contemporary linguists, folklorists and teachers.

Rosenplänter stressed the practical as well as the theoretical value of a knowledge of Estonian. His proposed introduction of at least two hours of Estonian language courses into the secondary schools of Estonia and Northern Livonia was revolutionary for those times. Without Rosenplänter's great contribution to the development of Estonian linguistics, and his warm and sympathetic attitude toward the Estonian language and people, the future work of Estonian folklorists, teachers, and writers would have been greatly hampered, if not entirely postponed, for decades. Rosenplänter's work in the fields of folklore and linguistics was only a part of his contribution to the development of a national consciousness. He was also an important figure in the development of Estonian schools, particularly in teacher education. In 1814 he oranized in Pärnu a three-year course for teachers in which, among other subjects, the technique of reading and writing Estonian was taught. He also helped to promote the theater in the Estonian language, and with his help several plays were produced in Pärnu.[2] He published many books in Estonian, mainly translations of German prose and poetry. He also compiled a bibliography of Estonian publications and books dealing with the Estonian language, *Bibliotheda Esthonica, das ist: chronologisches Verzeichniss aller estnischen, und über die estnische Sprache erschienene Schriften, 1553-1826*. The bibliography was never published.[3]

Rosenplänter was one of those few Baltic Germans who laid the groundwork for the activities of the Estophils. Though he was not a founder, his interest-provoking studies were partly responsible for the creation of a most important organization contributing to Estonian culture. This was the Estonian Learned Society, which was organized in Tartu in 1838 by a group of Baltic German Estophils, and later joined by a few Estonians with academic background. Among the most influential German members were Georg Merkel, J. W. Luce, and O. W. Masing.[4]

The cause for the creation of the organization was: (as stated by one German member)

. . . (of the German Balt). . . . in his love to his soil and to the Estonian people . . . a union of the educated, who wish to work together with the Estonian (people) . . . it was the first scientific body connecting the rest of the world in a scientific way with the Estonian people, with the Estonian language, the Estonian national beliefs, and with the Estonian mythology.[5]

The first statute of the Society declared the knowledge of the past and present of the Estonian people, language, literature to be fundamental.[6] This was the first step toward making the language one of science and literature, since at that time it was the language of the peasants. There were no educated Estonians who made much use of their mother tongue, even at home. The Tartu University until the creation of the Estonian Learned Society, did not have a single Estonian professor of the Estonian language. During the period 1842-1850 F. R. Fählman (1798-1850) was the only lecturer who taught the language.[7] At that time no materials existed in Estonian about the language or other topics of the culture, past or present. Nevertheless, it cannot be said that the Estonian people were on as low a cultural level as that of the Russian peasant. The desire for education, however slight the opportunities were, resulted in the steady growth of literacy. Evidence of the increase in literacy is the attempt of Otis Wilhelm Masing, a German, to publish an Estonian weekly paper, the *Maarahva Näddalaleht* (The Country-people's Weekly) during the years 1821-23.[8] The Estonian Learned Society was organized by nineteen persons, of whom eleven were German pastors, and only one (Fählman) was an Estonian. This is to the credit of the German intellectuals, who began serious scientific research in the Estonian language and culture and created a scientific Estonian vocabulary. It is not to the discredit of the Estonian people that its first scientific society was created by the Germans. There did not yet exist an homogenous Estonian intelligentsia which could perform this pioneering task, though there were already small groups of Estonian intellectuals. The German Estophils fulfilled an historical mission by pioneering in the field of Estonian culture, thus paying back a small fraction of the historical debt they owed the Estonian people after more than 600 years of suppression of its nationality.

One outstanding German member of the society was Ferdinand Johann Wiedemann (1805-1887). He was born in Haapsalu, Estonia and early showed his interest in languages. Wiedemann was graduated from Tartu University with a major in comparative linguistics (Greek, Latin, French, Italian, English, and Semitic languages). His interest in Estonian was aroused by O. W. Masing.[9] It was at a time when there was beginning to develop scientific interest in the Finno-Ugric languages, which started in Hungary and Finland and spread to Estonia through the publication in 1835 of the Finnish epic poem *Kalevala*. During his lifetime Wiedemann published many scientific articles about the Finno-Ugric languages and became the outstanding Baltic Finno-Ugric scholars of his time, being awarded membership in the Russian Academy of Science. Wiedemann's greatest contribution to Estonian culture was his studies in Estonian grammar: he published a three-volume Estonian-German dictionary, the best of his time, compiled from old manuscripts and earlier dictionaries. It is still considered one of the best, with a sound scientific basis. He also contributed studies of

Estonian mythology. Wiedemann's scientific work did not end with his linguistic studies. He was very successful in collecting Estonian folklore, which he published in the anthology, *Aus dem inneren und äusseren Leben der Ehsten,* in 1876, in St. Petersburg. The collection consists of more than 500 pages of proverbs, riddles, games, folktales, customs, and religious ceremonies.[10]

At the beginning of its activities, the Estonian Learned Society had a varied program. Meetings were held in the houses of members; discussions revolved around the history of the Estonian people and its poetry, traditions, and mythology. At the same time the members considered how to improve educational conditions and thus raise the cultural level of the people.[11] It was clear to the Estophils that, with the publication of scientific material, there should also be works of practical character aimed toward the education of the peasant. Of all tasks, one was considered most important: the collection and publication of the national epic, *Kalevipoeg.*[12] The aim of the reconstruction and publication of *Kalevipoeg* was twofold. First, it was hoped that a presentation of Estonia's heroic past would restore national pride and promote an interest in the continuation of the Estonian cultural heritage. Second, there was the desire to stimulate an interest in the Estonian people and culture among the western nations, especially among the Germans in the Baltic provinces, in order to destroy the common concept of the Estonian peasantry as a people without a culture.

2. Fählman and Kreutzwald—the Beginning of the Estonian Intelligentsia

Among the few Estonian students of Tartu University who joined the Estonian Learned Society, three were outstanding: Kristian Jaak Peterson (1801-1822), Frederick Robert Fählman 1798-1850) and Friedrich Reinhold Kreutzwald [pseudonym for Vidri Rei Rstimets (1803-1882).]

Peterson can be called the first Estonian intellectual to be conscious of his nationality, not ashamed of it before his German colleagues at Tartu University. Early in life Peterson showed great linguistic and literary gifts. Inspired by Rosenplänter's literary activites, he tried to write poetry in the Estonian language, a very unusual thing for those times, when every educated Estonian was trying to forget his past.[13] Peterson was a highly gifted linguist. He published several works on Estonian grammar, but his greatest contribution was to the study of Estonian mythology, in his annotated 1821 translation of the *Mythologia Fennica* (Finnish Mythology) by Christian Ganander. Peterson was the first to make use of Finnish myths in telling Estonian myths, thus helping later to create out of the names of the Finnish heroes, Väinämöinen, Ilmarinen and Lämmikälnen the Estonian equivalents of Vanemuine, Ilmarine and Lämmeküne which were later developed into Estonian mythical figures by Fählman and Kreutzwald.[14]

Friedrich Robert Fählman was free-born. His mother died while he was a child, and he was taken into the home of their landlord, a relatively liberal and humane noble by the name of von Patkull. Thus, at the age of seven, Fählman entered the German atmosphere. Though he never renounced his nationality, his attitude was in many ways very much that of a liberal, middle-class German. He was graduated from Tartu University with honors. During his student years he had to struggle with economic difficulties, gaining his living by tutoring. His intellectual interests were not limited to medicine. He attended lectures on philosophy, aesthetics, poetry, literature, comparative linguistics, and theology. During those years his *Weltanschauung* formed. Influenced by the ideas of Schelling as well as his own economic struggle, he became an empiricist, and thus opposed to theology. Throughout his life he was considered a "dangerous freethinker" by the clergy, and even after his death a friendly pastor tried to excuse him by telling of Fählman's actually "being a Christian by being just, modest and always helpful." [15] Fähllman was strongly influenced by the ideas of nationalism which were spreading over all of Europe during the 1820's. Especially appealing to him was the Estophilism of Rosenplänter and O. Masing and he became interested in acquiring mastery of the Estonian language. Through his interest in folk poetry, Fähllman became acquainted with Kreutzwald in Tartu in 1826. Though their first meeting might justly be called the beginning of an Estonian intelligentsia, it did not result in the creation of active interest in the cultural emancipation of Estonia. In 1842 Fähllman became the first Estonian to lecture on the Estonian language, and spent ever-increasing amounts of his time on studies in language and folklore. He intended to discontinue his medical practice, but he could not bring himself to resign from it. He continued to overwork himself until his death, in 1850, of tuberculosis. He had been susceptible to the disease since his 'teens.

Fähllman's contribution to the growth of the Estonian national ideas was considerable. As a liberal and an anticlerical, he denounced in all his writings the landlords and German pastors, and the exploitation of the peasants, as can be seen from his correspondence with Kreutzwald (which has been published) and Carl Robert Jakobson, two outstanding leaders of the Estonian people. His nationalism was not clear-cut, and his national consciousness was somewhat dim, owing to his German environment earlier in life. But Fähllman's idea of social justice put him on the side of his suffering Estonian brothers, and throughout his life he never failed to express his feelings on this subject. Kreutzwald's collection and publication of the national epic *Kalevipoeg,* which became a real force behind Estonian nationalism, was inspired by Fähllman.[16]

If Fähllman was the first professional intellectual among the Estonian people, a man to lay the foundations of an intelligentsia, Friedrich Reinhold Kreutzwald was the most im-

portant Estonian writer and folklorist of the nineteenth
century. Kreutzwald, the son of a poor peasant, spent his
childhood among peasants. He was impressed with their folktales and epics; they were the source of his rich and colorful
language of later life.[17] Influenced by the Estophils, he began
to write in Estonian very early. In 1826 he entered the medical faculty of Tartu University. But his interest was not
limited to medicine. He attended lectures on literature,
particularly that in German and the classical languages. In
Tartu he met Fählman. To the cherished ideas shared by the
two men, Kreutzwald contributed strong romantic feelings—
great love towards nature and the Estonian past.[18]

After graduation in 1832, Kreutzwald settled as a doctor
in the town of Võru, where he spent the rest of his productive
life. His writings were mainly of educational, pragmatic
character. He wrote such things as poetry, stories from peas-
ant-life, translations from German, and descriptions of other
countries. Kreutzwald was an enemy of alcohol: many of his
stories had a theme of anti-alcoholism. His greatest contribution was the collection and publication of *Kalevipoeg*—the
task of a lifetime, inspired by Fählman's great interest in
folk poetry and his collection of individual songs of *Kalevipoeg* Kreutzwald continued to collect pieces of the epic after
Fählman's death.[19] The printing of *Kalevipoeg* was a monumental task for the time, so great that no Estonian publisher
would undertake it. It was printed in Finland in 1862, together with the German translation, under the auspices of
the Estonian Learned Society. Far from being pure folk
poetry, the work was a literary conglomerate. Kreutzwald
adopted many elements from world literature, especially
from the Finnish folk epic *Kalevala*. But its effect upon the
Estonian reading public was tremendous: it reflected the
heroic past and hopes of the Estonians, and was invaluable in
fostering and strengthening a national spirit. This can be seen
from the concluding lines of the epic, (after the resurrection
of *Kalevipoeg*):

Kalevite poega pandi
Ratsul valge hobu selga,
Saadetie piiridelle
Väravad valkamaie
Sarvikuda sôitlemaie,
Kuri pääseks kütketesta.
Kui siis Kalevite poega
Veeres kaljuväravasse
Alla-ilma ukse ette,
Hüüetie ulevalta:
"Raksa Kaljut rusikaga"
Raske käega rabadessa
Loi ta kalju lihkemaie—
Aga käpp jäi kalju kütke,
Rusik kinni kivirahnu.
Sealap istub hobu seljas
Praegu Kalevite poega,
Käsi kütkes kalju kuljes,
Valvaö vahil väravada,
Kaitseb kütke teise kütkeid
Porgulastest puuetakse
Kahel otsal polend piiril
Ahelaida habrastada,
Kütkeid-a katkendella.
Jôula-ajal lahvad lülid
Peene hiukse karva paksuks;
Kui aga hüüab koidukukke
Vanaisa väravalta
Jôulupuha tulekuda,
Lähvad ahelate lulid
Järsku jälle jamedamaks.

Kalevipoeg püüab kätta
Vahetavehel vägevasti
Kaljuseinast lahti kista,
Raputab ja raksateleb
Maapohja mudisema,
Kuukaida koikumaie,
Mere valgelt vahutama;

Mana käsi hoiab meesta,
Et ei vahti väravasta,
Kaitsev poega põrgust Pääseks.

Aga ükskord algab aega,
Kus kõuk piirud kahel otsal
Lausa lähvad lõkendama;
Lausa tuleluki lõikab
Küll siis Kalev jõuab koju
Oma lastel õnne tooma,
Eesti põlve uueks looka.[20]

(When the Kalevide reached the rocky portal, a voice was heard from heaven, "Strike the rock with thy fist." He did so, and clove open the rock, and his right hand was caught in the cleft. Here he sits now on his horse at the gates of Põrgu [Hell], watching the bonds of others while bound himself. The demons attempted unceasingly to soften their chains by heaping up charcoal fagots around them but when the cock crows at dawn their fetters grow thicker again. From time to time, too, the Kalevide struggles to free his hand from foams; but the hand of Mana [the god of death] holds him, that the warder shall never depart from his post. But one day a vast fire will break out on both sides of the rock and melt it, when the Kalevide will withdraw his hand, and return to earth to inaugurate a new day of prosperity for the Estonians.) [21]

Kreutzwald became the living symbol of the national culture, since he was considered by many of his contemporaries as the Estonian writer who elevated the Estonian culture to a par with that of Western Europe. He and Fählman were the first two Estonian intellectuals in the European sense of the term, pioneering in the fields of literature and folklore, and supporting the cause of the Estonian cultural heritage, the revival of the Estonian past—without which there could not develop a national consciousness.

National consciousness was not only a matter of being conscious of something, but it was a matter of strength of character. For an Estonian who managed to break through the barriers of the peasant class and enter German culture and society, it required more than courage to go back to the Estonian past, something considered by most Germans as nothing more than rusticity. It was a matter of building up a new culture despite social stigmas of acceptibility of the German culture. Thus the struggle was one against conventionality— against a social environment much stronger than the small group of Estonian patriots.[22]

3. Changing Policies of the Estonian Learned Society (1860-1880)

With the publication of *Kalevipoeg* the first phase of the activities of the Estonian Learned Society came to an end. During this time (1838-1860) many changes had occurred within the society as well as in the country. By 1860 most of its founders had died, and a new generation grew up, with new ideals and new ideas about the purpose of the organization.

The new generation did not share in the romantic approach which appealed to the founders. Instead, they professed a frank approach to Estonian reality. We should not forget, however, that at that time the society still was mainly an organization of German Estophils, with only a minority of Estonian members. During the first few decades of its activities, the Society had aimed at collecting data on the past of the Estonian people: the members of the organization believed that they were saving the Estonian cultural heritage from being lost to mankind. It was, then, the purpose of the organization to save whatever could be saved. In other words, it was not so much love for the living culture as the idea of preserving the remnants of a supposedly dying culture. There were no didactic purposes behind the scholastic activities of the liberal German academicians of the 1840's and 1850's.[23] During the sixties, however, the conditions of the Estonian people were much different, culturally as well as economically, and the expectation of a quiet death for Estonian culture no longer existed. The people were eager to learn, to get education. The new generation of German liberals, particularly those active in the Estonian Learned Society, headed by the Baltic historian Carl Schirren, (1826-1910), regarded the national awakening of the Estonian people as naive and historically doomed to failure.[24] The co-workers of Schirren shared his opinion that the time had come for teaching the Estonian peasant how to lead a cultural life, which meant how to adopt the German culture. According to the men around Schirren, the road to education had to be that of the German language and German culture.[25] Schirren's influence upon his German Baltic contemporaries was strong. This was due to his impulsive, as well as impressive, personality, and to the strength of his conviction of the superiority of the German culture in the Baltic provinces. Schirren had a strong belief in the mission of the Germans in this area. This mission, Schirren believed, consisted in the preservation of the German way of life in the provinces, which was a result of the cultural, social and economic development of the region. This way of life, Schirren contended, was the primary force in the historic development of the provinces, and neither the Tsar nor the Russian government had any moral or legal rights to change the basic structure of the provinces or abolish them altogether.[26]

Schirren's Baltic conservatism did not stop him from accepting the liberal reforms in behalf of the Estonian peasants. For Schirren, however, it meant the improvement of economic and social positions of the peasants within the framework of the social order of the Baltic provinces. Schirren did not see in the emancipation of the peasants a step toward the full development of the Estonian culture, but rather a stepping-stone toward a gradual Germanization of the Estonian people, beginning with the Estonian intelligentsia. Such was the liberalism of Schirren and of many other members of the Estonian Learned Society. Thus the Estonian Learned Society was beginning to move toward a Germanization of the Estonian people. The well-meaning members of the society did not, however, consider the changes that had taken place within the people during those decades. Through the course of the emancipation, the beginning urbanization, the mass conversion to Orthodoxy and mass emigration, and the rebellions, the Estonian peasantry had improved its economic position, and was striving more and more toward becoming a class of independent small landowners. The activities of the early Estophils and the work of Peterson, Fählman and Kreutzwald left their marks upon the people. Also the steady growth of educational facilities in the villages and the introduction of the Estonian language in the curriculum of the parish schools resulted in the radical improvement of the peasant mentality. The peasant had changed from a manorial laborer to a seeker of self-sufficiency and economic independence, a man who read Estonian books and sent his children to school, where they learned history, religion, singing, reading and writing—taught in Estonian by Estonian teachers. All this the German Baltic liberals completely overlooked.[27]

Members of the Estonian Learned Society did not realize that the German language and culture were losing their position of being the only means of education for the peasantry. Though German culture was still much stronger than the young Estonian culture, and still attracted many an Estonian intellectual, it had lost its appeal to the masses, who had found a means of economic and cultural independence aside from Germanization. Thus there grew up a distinction between the goals of the society, and those of the Estonian people, in particular the young Estonian intelligentsia. Since the aims of the Schirren group ignored the demands of the Estonian people, the policy of the society was essentially unrealistic. It took the German members of the society some time to realize their mistake. After the majority realized it, they stopped pursuing the aim of educating the Estonian people; instead they concentrated on purely academic research and scientific publications.[28] This change of heart occurred during the 1860's. Such a change naturally caused some criticism from some Estonian members. Among them was Kreutzwald, himself an educator in a sense, who believed the purely academic pursuits of the society to be out of harmony with the original aims of the organization.

Since there were few Estonians with academic degrees, and since the beginning of the national movement was fostered by elementary school teachers, who did not have advanced education, little popular interest in the society developed. Thus the rift between the people and the society grew with the years. Owing to the academic character of the organization, most of its leaders were Germans. To mention only the most influential and active members during the second half of the nineteenth century, we should include: Professor Leo Meyer (1830-1910), who was professor of comparative linguistics at Tartu University from 1865-98 and the leader of the society for thirty years; Eduard Winkelmann (1838-1896), outstanding historian who compiled the first complete bibliography on Baltic history, the *Bibliotheca Livoniae Historica* (first published in St. Petersburg in 1870, and then revised and completed in Berlin, in 1878); [29] Professor Constantin Caspar Grewingk, (1819-1887) the first archeologist of the Baltic provinces; [30] and Ferdinand Johann Wiedemann, (1805-1887).[31]

Among the Estonian members of the Society, the most active and influential were Jakob Hurt (1839-1906), Michkel Weske (1843-1890), and Jaan Jung (1835-1900). Whatever differences existed between the views of Estonian culture and life held by the Estonian and by the German members of the society, the two groups never failed to cooperate in matters of collecting and publishing materials in the field of Estonian folklore and linguistics.

Great stimulus was given to the awakening of Estonian

national consciousness by one of the political leaders of Finnish nationalism, Yrjö Sakari Yrjö-Koskinen (1830-1903). The first great Finnish historian, he taught world history, and later Finnish, Russian and Scandinavian history at the University of Helsinki. He became a leading political figure in Finland and exercised great influence upon the development of nationalism in Finland. Yrjö-Koskinen early became interested in the Estonian emancipation. He read Estonian newspapers and wrote about Estonia for the Finnish press. He visited Estonia several times and developed connections with the leaders of the Estonian intelligentsia. After his return to Finland, he continued to correspond with Kreutzwald and others.[32] In his letters, and also in his articles in Finnish newspapers, Yrjö-Koskinen favored Estonian independence of the German economic and cultural hegemony. He stoutly demanded a voice in local affairs for the Estonian people. A sincere believer in the future of the Estonian culture, he encouraged the young Estonian intelligentsia to use their own language.

Thus the growing national consciousness received impetus from various sources, to create a small but energetic Estonian intelligentsia. A simultaneous growth of nationalism was taking place in the brother-country, Finland. Whereas in Finland, however, the people had never lost completely their feeling of national identity and the renaissance was inaugurated and fostered by the intelligentsia and went down rather easily from them to the peasant, the national awakening in Estonia sprang from among the peasantry, the poor village teachers and the *kösters;* its spirit inflamed the hearts of the emerging intellectuals, who, on the road to Germanization, found the way back to their people.

CHAPTER V

Urbanization, Agricultural Trends and Cultural Developments, 1830-1860

1. Beginnings of an Estonian Middle Class

The stormy 'forties resulted in several economic, religious and cultural changes in Estonia and Northern Livonia. The sporadic rebellious activities of the Estonian peasants and the following mass conversion of thousands to the Russian Orthodox Church with the hope of getting land greatly hampered the full application of the existing emancipation laws. The growing Estonian middle class and the trend towards Germanization of the young intelligentsia in the cities had their effects on cultural and economic developments in city and country during the following two decades.

Hoping to find land in Russia, thousands of landless Estonian peasants left their homes for Siberia and interior Russia, where they settled and built their own villages.[1] Many returned dissatisfied, but the restlessness in the villages continued, and the peasants eagerly sought escape from the burden of the manorial system. During the 1830's many peasants turned towards small trade in the country, an idea they got from traveling German merchants. Thus many peasants became itinerant tradesmen, walking from village to village and selling small wares to their fellow-countrymen on credit. The same merchandise could be bought in the

71

towns much more cheaply, but for the peasants in the villages it was much more convenient not to have to go to town, and they readily paid the traveling merchant's price.[2] The extension of credit often resulted in the financial ruin of the peasant-merchants, but in many cases the peddlers made good profits, and some even became rich. Such a trade, though, was harmful to the German businessmen in the cities, who could not afford to sell on credit.[3] Peasants who achieved some wealth through such a business completely lost their interest in agriculture. With their newly-acquired money they could pay their debts to the landlords or the community and settle in the cities. They were willing to consider anything that would make it possible to avoid paying the high taxes in the village, seeing their children taken into the army for life, and being dependent upon the will of the baron. Thus the beginnings of an Estonian middle class appeared in the cities during the 1830's.[4]

This trend of the peasants towards leaving the villages alarmed the nobility. After the peasants were freed from forced labor by the Russian government in 1865, and the system of monetary rent was put into effect, the nobles needed more hands on their farms. The migration of peasants into the cities and into Russia created a labor shortage on the farms and raised the wages for farmhands.[5] Some nobles favored legislation to stop the emigration, while some preferred letting the peasants go, but importing labor from other places, thus lowering the wages of the landless Estonians.[6]

2. Governmental Policies in the Country and in the Cities
     and German Reactions to it

Of great importance to a realization of emancipation was the decision of the Russian government in 1859 to sell crown land to their peasants. Until 1828 only the nobility had enjoyed the right of land ownership. Most of the land in Estonia and on the nearby island of Dagö belonged to the nobles; very little belonged to the crown.[7] On December 3, 1828, the government extended the right of land ownership to non-nobles. After the emancipation of 1816-19, the purchase of land by others than nobles had been forbidden, though still practiced in the case of the German middle class. The law of 1828 was directed towards legalizing such transactions for Estonian peasants as well as German burghers. Until 1858 the government placed so many legal obstacles in the way of the purchase of land by non-nobles that purchases were impossible. Thus the new proposal to sell land to non-nobles sounded very revolutionary to the frightened nobles, who still tried to preserve, in the face of changing social conditions, as many of their feudal rights as possible. The new proposal, therefore, aroused the strongest protest from the landowners. The intention of the Russian government was not to help the Estonian landless peasantry, but rather to enable the German middle class, and the landless nobility which did not belong to the *Ritterschaft,* to become landowners and thus create a landowning middle class. In such a way the Russian government hoped to weaken the privileged position of the Baltic nobility.[8] But in the eyes of the peasants, the noble landlord lost much of his prestige, though at the beginning the Estonian peasants did not benefit much from it.

The government speeded the emancipation of the peasants by liberalizing the passport law in 1863, giving the peasants the rights to get passports and leave the village.[9] For the village commune the government provided in 1866 a greater degree of self-government, which gave the peasants more freedom from their landlord.[10]

These two improvements gave great stimulus to the strengthening of the village as well as the migration of the peasants into the cities. In general they resulted in more freedom for the people and fortified their self-esteem. Such a development was variously viewed by Baltic Germans. The conservative majority, steadily losing its influence upon the liberal minority, was fearful of the rising tide of Estonian economic and political emancipation. Many liberal nobles gave more than moral support to such a development, actually helping their tenants by giving them longer loans, selling them land, and helping them to become economically self-sufficient.[11] Other German nobles did not believe in the ability of the Estonian peasant to become a landowner as the German peasant was. They did not think that the Estonians, used to overlordship and guidance for centuries, would ever be able to build a distinct peasant class in the German sense.[12] The Estonians, they argued, had no national pride or national consciousness.[13] Furthermore, they contended that since the Estonian people never had a historic past, they would never be able to develop national pride, social pride (that is, pride in their own peasant class). Such statements were uttered not only by the conservatives, but also by many well-wishing liberals who professed deep knowledge of the history and character of the Estonian people. Despite all those pronouncements, the critics of emancipation did not deny the ability of the Estonians to acquire education.[14]

Most pseudo-liberals believed that the peasants' education should be sufficient only to enable him to do his work better. As for his guidance, he should not look toward the young Estonian intelligentsia, which the Germans believed to be headed towards Germanization, but take example from the German landlords.[15] Such statements, however, could not stop the emancipation or turn back the historic development of Estonia. In time the German nobles realized that the Estonian peasant was no longer the slave-laborer of 1800, 1840, or even 1850. Times had changed; the nobles were forced to make a change, at least in tactics, if they wished to maintain any of their superiority. Thus many liberal nobles advised their conservative colleagues to modify their attitude toward the Estonian peasants and accept the latters' desire for economic independence.[16]

A step toward the development of an Estonian middle class was the abolition in 1866 by the Russian government of the privileges of the city guilds. This was the death-blow given at an opportune moment, to the remaining caste spirit in the cities. Now it became possible for the Estonian city-dwellers, who were socially on the lowest level, to compete with the German craftsmen on the open market. The road to an Estonian middle class was open, and the peasants did not miss their opportunity.

3. Further Developments in Public Education

During the 'thirties education had improved not so much through better teaching methods as through a growing desire for knowledge on the part of the peasants. After 1832 no illiterate would be accepted for religious confirmation. This was the basic educational law in Estonia.[17]

The new peasant laws of 1856 increased the responsibility of the communities toward public education. The requirement of an enrollment of 1000 for establishing a community school was reduced to 300. During those years new teachers' seminaries were organized in the provinces of Harjumaa and Virumaa. Nevertheless, the number of parochial schools, the next level above the village schools, did not increase much during the years 1830 to 1860, and only the best graduates from the community schools attended them. The curricula in the parochial schools were more diversified than in the community-schools. They consisted of reading, writing, studying the Old and New Testament, singing, the catechism, the Estonian language, drawing, geography, world history, and history of the Reformation. Where there were adequate teachers, Russian and German were also taught.[18] The rise in quality and quantity of public education lowered the illiteracy rate and paved the way for an advanced Estonian literature, which had begun its hesitant program at the beginning of the nineteenth century.

4. Early Estonian Literature

Books in the Estonian language had been written as early as the sixteenth century. These for the most part were translations from the catechism, made by German clergymen.[19] During the sixteenth and seventeenth centuries a number of books appeared, mostly of religious character, but, in some cases, educational. Their authors also were mainly German clergymen and the books were of didactic nature, intended for the use of the pastor in his community. The language of these publications was usually poor, Germanized Estonian, without regard for formal grammatical rules, which at that time did not exist. A turning point in the development of the language was the translation of the Bible into the Northern dialect of Tallinn (Reval) by the Moravian brethren in 1739.[20] Estonian literature continued to be of religious and didactic nature until the beginning of the nineteenth century. It was produced by educated Germans whose aim was to enlighten the ignorant peasants. Estonian was only a tool in the hands of the Germans, the only way they could reach the peasant.

Also aimed toward education, and not the revival of the language itself, were the works of the Estophils.[21] Their language, however, was greatly improved, since interest in Estonian was increasing, and voluminous works in the field of Finno-Ugric studies had appeared. The publications of the Estophils, religious as well as educational, stimulated a public demand for better reading and more interesting topics. By 1850 a considerable group of readers of Estonian had grown up.

The first writer of Estonian nationality was Kristian Jaak Peterson (1801-1822).* His poetry was predominantly romantic, though it contained elements of pseudo-classicism. In his songs he expressed the Estonian desire for freedom from want and oppression. His writings showed the influence of contemporary German Estophils, but his language was far superior to theirs in style and in strength of ideas. Peterson was widely read by his contemporaries, and his writings made an important contribution to genuine Estonian literature. Fählman (1798-1850) * and Kreutzwald (1803-1882) * continued in Peterson's footsteps. Though they did not produce literary works of high merit, they did much for the development of literature: being Estonians themselves, they knew the life and thought of the peasant, and could appeal more directly to the Estonian imagination and emotions than could the German Estophils.

Estonian literature, even in its early stages, became an important factor in moulding the mind, developing interest in the past, building up a large circle of readers, and in such a way sharing in the formation of an educated class. By 1850 the language of the young Estonian intelligentsia had begun to challenge the position of German as the proper tool for the emancipation.

CHAPTER VI

Turning Points in the Development of Estonian National
Consciousness and the Beginning of Internal Political Strife

It is difficult to measure the importance of individuals,
German as well as Estonian, in determining the course of
historical events in the provinces. It cannot be denied that
the German nobility as a class had the strongest impact. A
lesser, but still great force, was that of the Russian government, especially beginning with the second half of the nineteenth century. The Estonian people were relatively passive
until about this time. Owing to the reforms and resultant
economic and cultural development, the situation changed.
The Estonian people began to take an active part in shaping
its own destiny. The peasantry felt its growing independence
and acted accordingly. Some members of the intelligentsia
became more conscious of their responsibilities as leaders,
and backed by a nationally-conscious peasantry and middle
class, assumed the task of completing the emancipation at the
beginning of the twentieth century.

By the second half of the nineteenth century the Estonian
intelligentsia no longer needed the philanthropy of the Baltic
German nobility. It felt strong enough to take over from the
Estophils the enlightenment and leadership of the peasants.
During the decades of reform and national awakening leaders
from among the Estonian intelligentsia proposed different
solutions to the problem of landlord-peasant relationship.

Some believed in a peaceful, gradual evolution; others believed in a militant attack upon the practices of the nobles.

1. Jannsen and his Policy of Peaceful Means

The most outstanding of the first group was Johan Woldemar Jannsen (1819-1890). If anyone deserved the title of hero of the Estonian people, it was Jannsen. It is impossible to conceive of the events of Estonian emancipation, cultural as well as economical, without Jannsen. He so dominated every aspect of Estonian life that his life can be considered an integral part of the national awakening. Johann Woldemar Jannsen was born in 1819, in the district of Pärnu.[1] In his early youth he was very eager to learn, and he read everything he could get hold of. Estonian literature was then very limited —mostly religious books, catechisms, calendars, and very short articles concerning agriculture. Thus the personality of the impressionable young Woldemar was marked indelibly by the religious nature of his reading. Soon he learned the German language and began to read German books written for the enlightenment of the Estonian people. At the age of twelve he began to study under the local köster (sexton), a man named Koch, who taught him the usual subjects of the parochial schools. Jannsen stood out from among the other pupils on the basis of intelligence and ability to absorb knowledge. After the dismissal of Koch in 1838, Jannsen took over the school. In 1850 he settled in Pärnu, where he became principal and teacher in the newly organized city elementary school.

During his twelve years as a *köster* Jannsen had found the Estonian translations of church-songs very poor. By 1845 he had published his first volume of new translations, called *Seerni Laulukannel* (Singer of the Harp). This book aroused great interest, since it was the first publication of songs in literary Estonian. Second and third volumes appeared in 1851 and 1863. Meanwhile, Jannsen had also published many other, shorter, works of a religious nature. From his own childhood experience, though, he knew that a religious literature was not sufficient to educate and enlighten the Estonian people, but that a worldly literature was needed. Such a literature did not yet exist, and Jannsen decided that the time had come for it.[2]

The most important moment in Jannsen's life, and probably for the emancipation, came when he conceived the idea of publishing a newspaper. There Otto Masing had founded a newspaper, *Marahwa Näddala Leht* in 1821, but it collapsed for lack of readers after four years. In 1845 Jansen tried to get permission to publish a newspaper, but he was refused by the authorities, who believed that the people were not yet ready for a newspaper. Jannsen did not give up his idea of a periodical. He was determined to start with a yearly publication which would be a beginning in the direction of an Estonian press. In 1848 he published his first issue, the *Sannumetoja* (Newsbringer). There followed six more issues, containing stories for the most part humorous and enlightened, sometimes of historical nature. Some were translations from German; some were written by Jannsen himself. Most were stories reflecting the life of the peasants, and thus appealing to Estonian readers.[3]

Jannsen's publication caused a sensation among the Estonian population: this was the first time that such works had been printed. The success and popularity of his publication confirmed Jannsen's belief that the Estonian people were ready for a periodical press. After the inauguration of the liberal-minded Tsar Alexander II, Jannsen achieved his goal: permission for founding a newspaper, the *Pärno Postimees* (Pärnu Mailman), which he edited. While Jannsen was beginning his newspaper, an enterprising German, Laakman, started another newspaper in Tartu called *Maarahva Postimees* (The Country Mailman), under the editorship of a German clergyman, A. H. Willigerode (1816-1893). Though both newspapers had the same program, to educate and enlighten the Estonian people, there was a difference in their approach. Jannsen greeted his readers with the famous words: *"Terre, armas Eesti rahvas"* (Be greeted, dear Estonian people), telling them the good news that from now on the Estonian people would have its own press. The phrase *Estonian people* was used for the first time. It was a significant moment in the history of a people which had never been treated as a people, even by most of its own intelligentsia. For Laakman and Willigerode there was no Estonian people, but a peasant people, which they called *Talurahvas* (country-folk).[4] In contrast to Jannsen, they approached the Estonians with German condescension, supplying the peasant with information taken largely from German newspapers of little interest to the peasant. Jannsen published information taken from every-day life, using an understandable language, full of humor. While the *Maarahva Postimees* was a failure from its very beginning, the *Pärno Postimees* was a success. After two years Willigerode left the former, and an Estonian, Georg Thol, took over as editor. Thol, though knowing the Estonian language better, did not know the real interests of the people, and he also left the paper after half a year. A former pastor of Fennern by the name of Korber replaced Thol. He attempted to imitate Jannsen, but the newspaper steadily lost readers until 1859, when Laakman stopped it completely for lack of an editor.

Jannsen, through his newspaper, had become more and more popular. Realizing his success, he decided to publish his own newspaper. He choose Tartu, in the heart of Estonia, as the cultural center of the country on the basis of its university. Jannsen called his next weekly *Eesti Postimees* (The Estonian Mailman). Through this publication he spoke to the people and rallied the patriotic youth. The new name of *Eesti Postimees* was not the first expression of Jannsen's national consciousness. In 1861 he had popularized the name *Eesti Rahvas* in his third volume of songs, the *Eesti Laulik* (Estonian Songbook). Together with German songs translated into Estonian, Jannsen had published patriotic Estonian songs, which appealed to the national spirit in the Estonian people. Something which many Germans and *Kadakasaksad* [5] considered awkward and improper was becoming a symbol of rising Estonian nationalism: it was the picture of Jannsen, sold by him, inscribed with the following words (in translation): "Estonian man, remain under every dress and every name entirely true to your Estonian nationality; then you will be an honest man among your people." The portraits were bought by the thousands and hung on the walls of every Estonian home. [6]

2. The Song Festival of 1869

By the end of the 1860's Woldemar Jannsen had become the leading public figure of Tartu, beloved by the people and respected by his German contemporaries for his peaceful and calm attitude toward the Baltic nobility. Jannsen did not limit his literary activities to his newspaper, but continued to write on such diverse topics as poetry and practical advice to the peasants on problems of agriculture. During those years he cherished the idea of organizing an enterprise on a national scale which would unite the nationalistic forces of Estonia. Such an idea took shape in the organization of a national song festival in Tartu. While contemplating the festival, Jannsen discussed it with many of his Estonian and German friends. For the date Jannsen chose March 26, 1869—the semi-centennial of Estonian emancipation.

The realization of his dream was a great task for Jannsen. It required the cooperation of many people and a great deal of money. There was no building available in Tartu with the necessary capacity. There was not a single song-group organized in Estonia. Nevertheless, Jannsen believed in the great love of his people for music; he also knew that every church had its choir which sang German and Estonian songs.

As a beginning, Jannsen organized the first Estonian singing society, the *Vanemuine*, in June, 1865. Since active membership was small for the plans Jannsen had in mind, he introduced into the *Vanemuine* constitution a clause providing for inactive membership. This opened the *Vanemuine* to everyone. Jannsen organized lectures and began a library. In order to attract the youth, the society organized dancing parties. With Jannsen's able leadership and active participation the *Vanemuine* grew into a large organization and soon became the cultural center of Estonians in Tartu. When the proper time came, Jannsen decided to use the influence of the society in organizing the song festival.[7]

There was not much time to organize the festival for the anniversary of the emancipation. Preparations would require much time, and travel would be handicapped because of the conditions of the roads in the spring. There were no railroads. Due to the great number of participants, the meeting would have to take place in the open air; therefore, Jannsen postponed the festival until June.

Jannsen proceeded very carefully in securing support for his idea. He realized that the *Vanemuine* would not be able to undertake such a task alone, but that the support of a wide range of people from different groups would be needed. His plan was to organize a special committee made up of representatives of these groups. He appealed to the *kösters* and the pastors, since they controlled or influenced their communities. Further, the church choirs would be essential. Jannsen diplomatically proposed as head of the song-festival committee Adalbert Hugo Willigerode,[8] who was pastor at the mixed, Estonian-German St. Marien church in Tartu. Willigerode was respected by all groups in Estonia, and his support would mean that of all the clergy. Having published songs himself, Willigerode was a great lover of music, and was greatly interested in all phases of Estonian culture. He readily accepted the presidency of the committee.

The committee consisted of: J. W. Jannsen, vice-president;

A. H. Willigerode, president; J. Hurt, then a science teacher at the Gymnasium in Tartu; A. Eschscholz, at Tartu University; J. Mielberg, a student; A. F. Obram, a secretary of the city council of Tartu and vice-president of the *Vanemuine* society; A. Kordt, a potter; A. Luig, a köster at the St. Marien church; and many others. An appeal for participation was written and sent to all church choirs; more than 40 choirs with over 800 singers replied by promising their participation. The repertoire consisted of Estonian folksongs, German religious songs (translated into Estonian by Jannsen), and two Finnish songs. An open-air theatre was built. The educated and wealthy German burghers gladly lent the committee the use of property of the *Recource,* their summer-club, as the site of the theatre. In order to accommodate out-of-town people, the committee published an appeal for the aid of the citizens of Tartu; it received a warm response.[9]

The song-festival lasted from the seventeenth until the twenty-first of June, 1869, and it was a tremendous success. It united several thousand Estonians in a common enterprise for the first time in their history. Before returning to their homes, many stayed for private, friendly talks with old and new acquaintances, discussing their impressions of the festival days, making plans for future song-activities, and thinking about plans to further the cause of nationalism. There arose proposals to organize educational societies, which would work in different directions to enlighten and educate the common people. Everyone felt that there was no longer the distinction between many different small localities, but that a united Estonian people had just achieved success in a common enterprise. This despised peasant people had given evidence that it did not need the leadership of another nationality. Such was the conviction of all those who witnessed the festival, where the moral and cultural attributes of the Estonians came to light. The song festival commemorating the fiftieth anniversary of the Emancipation came to be regarded the birthday of the Estonian people.[10]

3. Jakobson and the Estonian Circle in St. Petersburg

The success of the song festival was weakened by the fric-
tion between two forces within the Estonian people. During
the first stages of planning for the festival, sharp criticism of
Jannsen and his supporters was voiced by a more militant,
nationalistic group, headed by Carl Robert Jakobson (1841-
1882).[11] He belonged to a second group of Estonian intellectuals, to whom Jannsen's slow and peace-loving policy was
anathema.

Born in Tartu, Jakobson was the son of an ambitious
Estonian cobbler, who himself became a *köster* and then a
teacher of a community school. Jakobson received his earliest
education from his own father. After graduating from the
community school, he continued his education in the Valga
(Walk) Teacher's Seminary. After his father's early death,
he took over the community school he had attended as a boy.
Being insulted by a German noble, Jakobson left the school
and eventually arrived at St. Petersburg. There he studied
privately and received a high school teacher's diploma. He
made the acquaintance of an outstanding Estonian, Johan
Köhler, an artist at the court of the Tsar.[12] At that time there
was a sizeable Estonian colony in St. Petersburg. Many Estonians there reached high social positions—notably Köhler;
Philip Jakob Karell (1806-1886),[13] the private doctor of Tsar
Alexander II; Nikolaus Friedrich Russow (1828-1906),[14] a
government worker; Dankmann, a schoolteacher; and Alexander Jurjev, a court-counsellor.[15] The members of this outstanding group became spokesmen for the Estonian people at
the St. Petersburg court. Their activities were inspired by
those of the St. Petersburg Latvian group, which published
a Latvian newspaper, the *Peterburgas Awises,* under the
energetic leadership of Kristian Valdemars (1825-1891).[16]
Valdemars, studying at Tartu University, concentrated
around himself many students of Latvian origin who discussed literary and cultural problems pertaining to the Lat-

vian and Estonian peoples. Valdemars published books on the abilities of the Latvians and Estonians in the field of navigation, which caught the attention of the Russian government.[17] In another book *Baltische, namentlich livländische Bauernzustände,* (Leipzig, 1861), Valdemars strongly criticized the agricultural situation prevailing in the Baltic provinces. A translation into Estonian, though never printed, was widely read in manuscript. In *Petersburgas Awises,* Valdemars published many articles criticizing the conditions of the Latvian and Estonian peasants. His strong anti-German attitude evoked protests from German nobles and clergymen, and his newspaper was forbidden.

During its brief existence the *Petersburgas Awises* greatly stimulated the Estonian colony in St. Petersburg.[18] Having great influence in governmental order, the more active members of the Estonian colony brought to the attention of the government the deplorable conditions in Estonia. Some of their information was first-hand, acquired in visits to their homes. In their attitude toward the Baltic nobility they were diametrically opposed to Jannsen's mild policy. It was no wonder that, living in St. Petersburg, working for the Russian government, and having connections with the court, Jakobson, Köhler and the others saw in the Russian government their only natural ally against the Baltic German nobility. Thus they strongly rejected the whole idea of Jannsen's song festival in association with the Germans; they also objected to the celebration of the date, since they considered emancipation as not yet realized.

Jakobson was in Tartu at the time of the song festival. Though the success of the festival was obvious, it did not shake his negative attitude or that of Köhler, Jurjev, and Karell. Strongly anti-German and anti-clerical, constantly swarmed by complaining letters from Estonian peasants, Jakobson and his friends criticized the song festival as a glorification of the Germans rather than an aid to the Estonian cause.[19] The St. Petersburg colony openly accused

Jannsen of collaborating with the nobility and being sub-
servient to them. It is very difficult, though, for us to judge
the validity of their criticism; we must consider the fact that,
except for short visits, the Estonians in St. Petersburg did not
actually experience conditions in Estonia. It was much easier
for them, having good positions in St. Petersburg, to criticize Jannsen for his peaceful tone. It was much more difficult
for Jannsen and his group to be militant.

4. Jakobson's and Jannsen's National Ideologies and the Latter's Agricultural Activities

Prior to 1870, Jakobson had published many articles in
Jannsen's *Eesti Postimees*. But the two men conflicted concerning Estonian school programs. Jakobson, being anti-
clerical, insisted upon the lessening of the amount of religious instruction in the schools. He considered the strong
influence of the pastors, particularly Germans, as hindering
Estonian cultural growth. From educational problems Jakobson proceeded to general problems. He considered the problem of education as only part of the emancipation question.
He realized that in order to promote education there should
be sufficient economic improvement. In this respect he
thought along the same lines as Jannsen, who also realized
the importance of the economic stabilization of the peasantry.
But Jannsen believed in a peaceful transition of the peasant-
renter into the land owning class, while Jakobson did not
believe in such a solution.

New agrarian laws were slowly but steadily giving results.
New banks were created for the purpose of helping the peasant to buy his land. Estonia, however, showed the slowest
rate of land-purchase of all the Baltic provinces.[19] This
could be partly explained by such conditions as the closeness
of the houses in Estonian villages, poor soil, and unfavorable
climate—but it was also very much due to poverty.[20]

Jannsen did much to overcome the handicaps of the peasant. The success of the song festival gave him impetus to organize additional activities. Since the festival had shown the ability of the Estonian people to organize cultural enterprises, Jannsen and others fixed upon economic improvement as the foundation for cultural progress. Concern for the national economy was identical with concern for the peasants, since they constituted more than 95% of the population. Therefore, an early question was the organizing of agricultural societies to teach the peasant improved farming techniques. After the abolishment of manorial labor in 1866, the peasants had more time to devote to their own land.

Jannsen set to work immediately after the abolition of the manorial system. He secured the help of a liberal noble, Hermann von Samson-Urbs, the secretary of the German Livonian Economic Society *(Livländische Ökonomische Sozietät)*. Jannsen began to edit and publish the *Eesti Põllumees* (The Estonian Peasant), an Estonian supplement to the German *Baltische Wochenschrift*. In this publication Jannsen printed letters from peasants on different agricultural problems. He also wrote articles of advice on many aspects of agriculture. His popular style aided him in developing on the part of the peasants great interest in improvement. The *Eesti Põllumees* became very helpful in solving the peasants' daily problems. The culmination of Jannsen's agricultural activities was the organization of the *Estonian Agricultural Society (Eesti Põllumeeste Selts)* in Tartu, in July, 1870. This organization was to play an important part in the renaissance of the peasant.

The German Attitude Towards Estonian National Awakening During the Years 1840-60

The German nobles looked with varied reactions upon the transformation of the Estonian peasant from a manorial laborer into an independent farmer. Accustomed to see in him the ignorant, uneducated slave, they were surprised to find him so ambitious in working towards economic independence. Most of the Baltic nobles did not believe that the Estonian, after 600 years of bondage, would be able to develop a middle or upper class. They were surprised to see the rise of such classes in the cities and towns of Estonia.

During the 1860's the opinion still flourished, despite acknowledgement of the peasant's intelligence and ability, that Germanization was his only means to culture.[21] One proponent of Germanization, for instance, recorded his belief that Germanization was no misfortune. Estonians, he pointed out, would share this loss of identity with some other peoples which had disappeared in the course of time or changed into other nationalities: [22]

. . . There is an open road for the Estonians . . . towards higher education and, with it, transfer into another social stratum; but while making such a step, they will leave their nationality and enter another—in this case, . . . the local German culture—and become Germans. . . . Both [Estonians and Latvians] do not lose anything; rather, they gain by leaving their peasant class . . . The Estonians are not even peasants, though they till the earth. They are rather manorial workers, servants, . . . despite their numbers . . . Since the Estonians do not own the land they till, but rent it from the German landlord, who can evict them after the contract terminates, they belong to the proletarian class.[23]

The author of this statement, however, did not consider the prevailing situation normal. He and many other liberal nobles believed that such a situation halted the economic development of the country. The unwillingness of the majority of nobles to sell their land to the peasants, despite the credit-banks which were created for this purpose, was considered sabotage of the land-reforms not only by the Estonians themselves, but by the liberal wing of the Baltic nobles.

Such were the conditions at the beginning of the second

half of the nineteenth century. That the development of the Estonian peasants did not follow the path of Germanization, as hoped by some well-meaning liberals, but continued along the path of Estonian culture, was due to the activities of the Estophils and men like Peterson, Fählman, Kreutzwald, Jakobson and Jannsen.

CHAPTER VII

National Awakening and National Activities

The final abolition of the manorial system in 1868 and the growth of the rights of the Estonian peasant gave strong impetus to the economic and cultural progress of the peasant communities. There particularly grew among the Estonians the desire for more and more education. During the liberal decade of 1860-1870, the Estonian national spirit rose against Germanization. Some German liberals supported the movement; some considered Germanization "as the means of fostering the equality of the Estonians with their former masters." [1]

The era of Alexander II saw a new Russian policy towards the Baltic provinces; it was the beginning of Russification. A strong attack upon the dominance of Germandom and of German culture in the provinces by the leading Russian Slavophils Katkov and Samarin added to the anti-German attitude. [2]

In the pages of the conservative Slavophil newspaper *Moskovskaia Gazeta* (Moscow Gazette) and in Samarin's *Okrainy Rosii* (Russia's Borderlands) the Baltic nobility were accused of preserving the medieval privileges of the nobility, oppressing the native Estonian and Latvian populations, and advocating the complete Germanization of the provinces, which would ultimately bring political separation from Russia. In reply, the German Balts defended themselves in the

pages of their own press and, when it was not possible because
of censorship, in publications from Germany.[3]

1. The Samarin-Schirren Controversy

Jurii Samarin in his *Okrainy Rossii* (Russia's Borderlands),
delivered the strongest blow against the Baltic Germans. The
book, published in Prague in 1868, gives a detailed account
of the status of the German Balts and their political and
cultural monopoly in the Baltic provinces.

Samarin accuses the Germans of misusing the Articles of
Capitulation of the Baltic German *Ritterschaften* in order
to perpetuate their six hundred-year-old privileges in the
Baltic provinces.[4] The author begins with a criticism of the
Balts' concept of their privileges which the nobility derived
from the Capitulations. He points out that when the Russian
government introduced the Provincial Laws for the Baltic
region in 1845 it automatically abolished the privileges of
the Baltic nobility.[5]

Samarin attacks the Baltic nobility for misleading public
opinion through shrewdly published excerpts from the provincial privileges granted them by Peter I and confirmed by
Paul and Catherine II.[6] Furthermore, he accuses the Baltic
Lutheran Church of suppressing all attempts of the Estonian
and Latvian peasants to join the Russian Orthodox Church.[7]
The reforms and the economic improvement of the peasants
the author attributes not to the good will of the Baltic nobility, but to the determined attitude of the Russian government, and the latter's interference in Baltic affairs against the
will of the nobles.[8] Samarin sharply denounces the nobles'
claim of helping the peasants purchase the land through the
credit banks. This impression, he contends, is absolutely
wrong, since the ways in which the peasants supposedly can
buy the lands are closed to them in practice owing to the
refusal of the landlords to sell their lands; in other words,
the credit banks can help the peasants only if the landlords

agree to sell. This, he stresses, happens very rarely, and the conditions under which the peasants can buy the land from the nobles are extremely unfavorable, and put them, if they agree to buy, into almost perpetual debt to the nobles.[9]

In the following chapter Samarin tries to justify the introduction of the Russian language in the school system. The reasons for such an action lie in having a number of civil servants for the Russian administration who would know the Russian language. Since the Baltic intelligentsia (the Germans as well as the native Estonians and Latvians) are the future servants of the state, it is of utmost importance to prepare them for their future work by making them study the Russian language.[10] The author continues by showing how the Russian government has helped to promote the economic development of the Baltic provinces; he adduces as an example the abolition of guilds and introduction of free enterprise.[11] Furthermore, he shows how the introduction of juridical reforms has brought about an improvement in the legal position of the Estonians and Latvians, giving them for the first time a voice in some affairs where they had often been abused by the nobles.[12]

In strong words the author denounces the nobles' attempt to Germanize the Latvians and Estonians by helping to create a small, wealthy elite among the Latvian and Estonian peasantry, which would quickly adopt the German culture and become good Balts. Such a policy of Germanizing a small segment of the native population, he contends, was adopted when the Baltic nobility realized the impossibility of changing the culture of the whole native population; once the small group had been assimilated, it would, in turn, lead the rest of the Latvians and Estonians toward Germanization.[13]

In the final part of his book, Samarin summarizes the position of the Baltic nobility, their adherence to their medieval privileges, and their outcry against the interference of the Russian government in the affairs of the Baltic provinces. He

comes to the conclusion that the Russian government has not
broken contract with the nobility; it has eliminated their
privileges in order to restore justice to the native population,
oppressed for centuries by their German masters.

The Russian government has been more conscious of the
duty of improving conditions in the Baltic provinces, the
author concludes, by introducing new laws. If those new
laws have hurt the privileges of the Baltic nobles, it is the
fault of the nobles for being behind the times.[14]

Jurii Samarin's book exploded like a shell amidst the Baltic
nobility. It was the strongest condemnation of the Baltic
Germandom, and it aroused sharpest protest from them. A
reply came from Carl Schirren, an outstanding Baltic historian and champion of the Baltic nobility and its culture.
In his *Livländische Antwort an Herrn Juri Samarin,* published in Leipzig in 1869, Schirren sarcastically replied to
Samarin's accusations. As his basic concept Schirren stressed
and defended the idea of the privileges granted to the nobles
at the beginning of the eighteenth century.[15] He pointed out
that those privileges had a good effect in the Baltic provinces,
and that the Russian empire could never complain of the
loyalty of the nobles. He accused the Russian government
blocking willfully and without provocation the natural development of the Baltic provinces by forcing upon them
unnatural laws, organizations and reforms.[16] Whatever accusations Samarin brought against the nobles, Schirren
always returned to the basic privileges, and from this point
of view attacked Samarin. At the end of his book Schirren
concluded that the Baltic nobles were the only legal heirs to
the Baltic provinces; that the Capitulations of 1710 must be
the foundation of all the future policy and development of
the Baltic provinces; and that the Baltic nobility had the
right and the duty to continue their struggle against the destruction of their age-old institutions, the very foundation of
their future existence. Schirren professed loyalty to the Tsar
and the Russian government, but at the same time he con-

cluded: "The German people and their descendants in this land and this land for the German people and their descendants—this is the sum of all Capitulations." [17] Into this sentence Schirren put the very essence of his conservatism.

His answer did not end the polemics, but only added fuel to the strife, which continued with undiminished fervor between the Slavophils and the champions of the Baltic nobility. For Schirren, however, his book was expensive: it cost him his professorship at Tartu University, thereafter he voluntarily left the provinces and went to Germany, where he continued in the pages of the conservative German press to denounce the Russification policy.

During the reign of Alexander II the accusations of the Slavophils did not find much governmental support, though Alexander himself was not opposed to peaceful Russification of the Baltic provinces. The Slavophils' attacks upon the privileges of the Baltic nobles indirectly aided the Estonian people. The Estonian middle class, the well-to-do peasantry, and the intelligentsia, encouraged by the attacks, sought more economic and political independence at the expense of the nobility and the German middle class.

2. The German Attitude towards Estonian Higher Education

With the improved economic situation of the 1860's, and with the peasants' penetration into the towns and cities, the demand for facilities for higher education in the Estonian language became stronger.[18] Even the increasing number of elementary schools was no longer adequate. Some German liberals sympathized with the demands of the Estonians for higher education and supported them publicly.[19] There were, however, many German Balts who believed that the building of secondary schools in the Estonian language would be too expensive and too much intellectual effort would be lost in writing Estonian textboks, preparing teachers, etc. There was, they said, available German culture, with German high schools and books at the disposal of the Estonians who were eager to learn.[20] They believed that:

There [did] not exist an Estonian . . . literature which could measure up to the German, which therefore could not take the place of German literature without harming the quality of school education. Nor do we have enough teachers who would be able to transform science from the German into Estonian from without the greatest harm to science. For there is not even an Estonian scientific language . . . Our teacher, be he of German or Estonian origin, is always German-educated . . . If today we wished first an Estonian literature and then the corresponding teacher force to shape and educate with it, we should hold back our general education for decades.[21]

The anonymous author of this statement expressed the belief that the Estonian should be allowed to use his native language in his daily life. He did not believe, however, that Estonian would ever be more than a peasant language. He concluded, therefore, that there would never be a highly developed Estonian literature.[22]

Such an opinion was not unique, but represented a large segment of the Baltic Germans. Many of them were well-meaning persons who believed that the only way for an Estonian to become educated was to adopt German culture. But the Estonian peasant no longer dreamed of leaving his community, going into the city and becoming a *saks* (as the peasants called the Germans). Now he wanted his children to be educated Estonians rather than educated Germans.

3. The Alexander-School Movement and the Viljandi Peasantry

Despite high prices set by the landlords, the peasants worked hard and, with the help of the *Creditkassen* (Peasant Credit Banks), some of them were able to purchase lands. During the decade following complete emancipation (1868) a small but active group of wealthy peasants emerged in the

southern province of Viljandimaa, where the soil was better.
There a sturdy, hard-working, and economically independent
peasant class developed. There the Estonian people found its
strongest fighters for national emancipation.

The Viljandi peasants were especially grateful to the Tsar-
Liberator, Alexander II, for their position, and they wished to
perpetuate his name. This idea merged with another idea
current in the minds of the Viljandi group: the building of
an Estonian high school, where all the subjects would be
taught in the Estonian language. The name they intended to
use was *Alexandri-Kool* (The Alexander School). And they
did more than talk about the project; in 1863 they collected
340 rubles and sent for the advice of the Estonian Learned
Society.[23] From the Society they learned that the establishment of such a school would require at least 100,000 rubles—
a sum beyond the imagination of the Estonian population.
Carl Schirren, president of the Estonian Learned Society,
added the disheartening advice "that the best and happiest
thing for them would be to be turned into Germans." [24] This
attitude on the part of a supposedly pro-Estonian organization
greatly disappointed the Viljandi group, but it did not stop
them from continuing to work toward the realization of their
dream, an Estonian institution of higher learning. This disappointment in the good will of the Germans was a blow to
Jannsen and to all advocates of peaceful cooperation with the
German, and strengthened the position of Jakobson and the
radical nationalists who followed him in his attacks upon the
Baltic Germans.[25]

From Viljandimaa the idea of the Alexander School
spread all over the country. It found a strong promoter in the
person of a young Estonian student at Tartu University,
Jakob Hurt (1839-1907).[26] The delegates from Viljandimaa
met Hurt in Tartu and from then on Hurt gave all his
energy toward organizing the Alexander School. Professor
Hans Kruus, the foremost Estonian historian, summarizes
events in the following way:

And in this respect the St. George day (April 24) of 1863 and the day following it have an important place in the history of the Estonian national emancipation.

But the day on which the delegation from Viljandimaa took part in the board meeting of the Estonian Learned Society had yet another important effect on the further development of the Estonian national movement. At this meeting the men from Viljandimaa got acquainted with the schoolmaster G. Blumberg and an undergraduate called Jakob Hurt, with whom they spent on the same day, "some love-filled hours and evening,". At this friendly sitting the men from Viljandimaa received many a useful hint for their enterprise and, what is more, encouragement for its realization. In those hours the first important contact was established between the more wide-awake, educated country people and farmers of Paistu and Tarvastu on the one hand, and the more nationally minded educated townspeople of Tartu on the other. The first kindled and he, henceforth, became an active supporter of the Estonian Alexander-School idea. During those hours of conference on the evening of April 24, 1863, one of the corner-stones to Jakob Hurt's development into a national leader was laid, which proved of the utmost importance to the subsequent development of the national movement in its entirety. Standing before his final examinations at the university, that son of a poor Himmaste village schoolmaster was, it is true, strongly rooted in the Estonian soil.

Being a member of the aristocratic German students' organization "Livonia," he had yet kept in touch with his poor home. But there were yet waiting for him many temptations apt to draw him from his home and people. It is now futile to speculate whether or not, without the great national enterprise in the offing, he would have yielded to those temptations.

Yet it is highly probable that Hurt, who, by nature, was more of a scholar than a warlike leader of men, would otherwise have devoted himself solely to philological and folkloristical pursuits. Now, however, bound up with the development of the Estonian Alexander-School idea, Hurt also developed into an Estonian politician and ideologist. And the fact that he became, in the first place, one of the foremost promoters of the idea of an Estonian school with instruction in the mother tongue is due chiefly to the close contact with the men from Viljandimaa established on April 24, 1863.[27]

It is hard to disagree with Professor Kruus' opinion that the conception of the Alexander-School marked the most important point in the beginning national movement. It was the first action of the Estonian peasantry in collaboration with its middle-class and intelligentsia—the whole people were united in their effort toward a national goal. The issue was not closed for another twenty years. There obviously were other turning points in the national awakening of the Estonian people, such as the bloody revolts in Mahtra and Harju, and the less aggressive but not less effective Song Festival. It is, therefore, difficult for us to single out the establishing of the Alexander-School as the turning point, but it certainly was one of those historically far-reaching events in the development of a people, which shape its character and direct its historic path.

In Professor Kruus' eyes, the event shares importance with the petitions and delegations the peasants sent to the courts of St. Petersburg (to be mentioned in greater detail later). Those petitions, the historian believes, culminated in the collective demand by the Viljandi peasants to Tsar Alexander II in the autumn of the year 1864. This petitioning stemmed from the social changes in the village and from the difficult transition period of the money-rent. Though it was of social origin, it consolidated the Estonian peasants in their struggle against another social class, identified by them as that of the German nobles.

4. The Struggle Between the Radicals and the Conservative Estonian Nationalists and the Formation of an

Estonian National Ideology

More than anyone else, Carl Jakobson realized the economic needs of the peasants as fundamental for emancipation. Since he could no longer express his views in Jannsen's *Eesti Postimees,* Jakobson tried to organize his own newspaper. Through the influence of his friend Johan Köhler, he finally got permission to begin the *Sakala,* which first appeared in 1878.

The *Sakala* turned a new page in political developments. It was sharp in its anti-German attitude and in strong contrast to Jannsen's peaceful *Eesti Postimees.* Jakobson broke with the belief of Jannsen that it was still possible to maintain good relations with the nobility while achieving full emancipation. Jannsen was not susceptible to the new Russian liberal stream, since he did not believe that the future of Estonia could be promoted by this trend. A bitter political fight began between the two newspapers. At first such outstanding Estonian national leaders as Kreutzwald, Hurt, and Michkel Weske joined forces with Jakobson.[28] But soon Hurt disagreed with Jakobson and the latter's anti-clerical position. In his defense Jakobson denied being against religion. He did insist, however, that the reactionary German clergy was a bad influence. What he was fighting for was an end of the privileges of the Germans, and for equal rights for his own people with the Germans. This political struggle brought about a sharp split in the Estonian national forces. It greatly handicapped the work of the Alexander-School committee, from which Hurt was expelled. Finally Jakobson's enemies managed to get his *Sakala* forbidden by the Russian authorities as socialistic. This charge was far from true, since Jakobson had never been a socialist, nor did he ever express socialistic sympathies. Under such pressure, Jakobson decided to make peace. He never fulfilled his decision: he died suddenly of complications resulting from a neglected cold.[29]

The death of Carl Robert Jakobson was a tremendous blow

to Estonian political maturation. He died on the threshold of a new era: that of forced Russification by Alexander III—a move which Jakobson and many of the St. Petersburg circle hoped would aid their struggle against the nobles. His death did not stop the growth of nationalism, the peasants' striving for economic independence, or the improvement of educational conditions. The dam of feudalism was broken and the tide swept away the remains of it. But the closing of the *Sakala,* the death of Jakobson, and the increasing pressure of the Russian government upon the Baltic provinces greatly delayed the cultural emancipation of the Estonian people. The new leaders, Hurt and Michkel Weske, were less militant, and tended toward compromise with the nobility in order to avoid clashing with them. None was a fighter like Jakobson.

Hurt's great contributions to the Estonian cause were his work in folklore, his leading role in the Alexander School movement, and his organization of the *Eesti Kirjameeste Selts* (Estonian Literary Society) in 1872. Settled in St. Petersburg in his later years, he stayed away from active participation in Estonian life. Jakob Hurt was a gifted linguist and by his whole character rather an academician than a political contestant. He often showed great friendship for the Baltic Germans, for which he was sharply criticized by Jakobson and the radical nationalists. Later, however, he joined forces with Jakobson, writing for the *Sakala* and defending Jakobson's view during the Alexander School movement.[30] Hurt's close cooperation with the radicals did not last for long. Basically the man was a scholar, and he spent the rest of his life in research, in writing and the teaching of linguistics.

Some historians consider Hurt the founder of the national ideology. Hurt propagated among his people the idea of the lasting value of the Estonian culture. Again and again he stressed his belief that the Estonian people did not cease being a nation during the six hundred years of slavery. He insisted upon a proud continuation of the Estonian language and literature. In the past of the people, Hurt saw the strong-

hold of the Estonian nation. During his life he published
many articles and books on Estonian history such as *Pildid
imama sündinud asjust* (Pictures from the Birth of a Nation),
(1879). In the ancient Estonians' stubborn adherence to their
culture, in their desperate struggle for freedom, Hurt saw
the sources of his people's growing strength. For this, Hurt
can be called the founder of an Estonian national ideology,
for which he stood all his life.

5. Education, Literature and Social Activities: 1860-1880

The 'sixties and 'seventies witnessed a tremendous change
in the Estonian provinces. Economic improvements and the
growing middle-class and intelligentsia led to the desire for
more and better education. In 1883 Hugo Treffner founded
the first private Estonian *Gymnasium,* in Tartu. Primary
schooling also expanded. Though the first schools were for
boys only, the first institute for girls' was founded in Pärnu
in 1880, under the leadership of an outstanding woman
writer and educator, Lily Suburg. The growth of parochial
schools in the cities and large village communities was of
significance in elevating national spirit.[31]

There was no difference between private and public schools
with respect to their programs, but, since the public schools
were controlled and administered by Germans, and the private Estonian schools were led and maintained by Estonians,
the role performed in fostering Estonian nationalism was
much greater in the latter. While public schools were teaching
the children the three R's, they worked in the German spirit
and under German influence, and tended to promote the
Germanization of the Estonian intelligentsia. This danger of
Germanization was especially prevalent in the city schools,
where the wealthy peasant children were studying. The fact
that the Alexander School idea signified steering away from
Germanization explains its tremendous appeal. The increase

in wealth among the Estonian population and the growth of public and private education created a demand for better books and periodicals. In the eight-year period from 1856 to 1863, 366 Estonian books were published. Twenty years later, the publication rate was approximately twice that of the earlier period: In 1883 and 1884, 154 books and brochures were published.

The growth of nationalism received added force from Estonian Romantic literature, with its strongest representative, Lydia Koidula, the daughter of Voldemar Jannsen, (1843-1886) [32] and such less-gifted poets as Michkel Weske, (1843-1890) [33] and Friedrich Kuhlbars (1841-1924) [34]. Their poetry, full of lyrical expressions of love for their country, its people and past, greatly stimulated the reading public. The Romantic school did not achieve high literary quality, except for the outstanding poetry of Lydia Koidula, but it utilized the Estonian past and gave the reading public ample food for thought.

The activities of writers and poets, publicists and newspapermen found expression in the *Eesti Kirjameeste Selts* (Estonian Literary Society, founded during the 1860's). Under the able leadership of Jakob Hurt and Carl Jakobson, the organization helped to build a homogenous Estonian intelligentsia, with a strong national consciousness of its own. The Estonian Literary Society fostered the publication of yearbooks, school texts, calendars, and science books for the enlightenment of the public. By these means it fostered the development of the young Estonian literature. Of some importance for the improvement of literature. was the adoption of Roman characters for the Estonian language, previously printed in Gothic.

The creation in Tallinn in 1865 of the musical society *Estonia,* sister organization to *Vanemuine,* and the formation of agricultural societies in smaller Estonian towns like Viljandi, Pärnu, and Narva cemented a strong collective feeling of national belonging. By the beginning of the

1880's a distinct national consciousness had crystallized. Many developments as well as many outstanding national leaders were responsible for such developments. There was nationalizing force in Voldemar Jannsen's newspaper activities, his building of an Estonian press, and his organization of the *Vanemuine* Society and the song festival; the same force was in Hurt's firm belief in the historic mission of the people and his high esteem of the past; it was in the political and literary activities of Carl Robert Jakobson, culminating in his three patriotic speeches to the Estonian people.[35] This force was present likewise in the collective action of the Viljandi peasants in presenting their grievances to the Tsar. Those protests reached the Tsar with the help of the Estonian intelligentsia, which drew up the grievances and demands of the peasantry. Thus there developed a common language of the two classes and a common aim: improvement of the conditions of the Estonian people.

6.   The German Attitude Toward the Alexander School and the Cultural Emancipation of the Estonian People, 1860-1880

During the two decades following the introduction of monetary rent, the attitude of the nobility changed in many respects. Many liberals looked favorably upon the energy and enterprise of the peasants in building up their own farms. They really believed that the improvement of the lot of the peasants would improve the German-Estonian relationship, and favor the economy of noble and peasant alike. Those liberal Germans considered the urge of the Estonian population towards education in their own language as absolutely justified.[36]

Some liberals, however, were sorry that the time was past for the easy Germanization of Estonian people. They believed, nevertheless, that they should show their helpful attitude toward Estonian cultural emancipation. An anonymous

German Balt wrote on this problem: "A new but significant perspective in the field of education was offered to us in recent times, in a long appeal which would by way of collection procure the means to the foundation of a higher public school in an exclusively Estonian language of instruction." [37]

This was written in connection with the collection of money for the Alexander School, carried on not only among the Estonians, but continued among the more liberal-minded Germans. Many of those Germans, considering such a project of benefit for the Estonian people, gave financial aid.[38] However, the same liberal author felt:

But a higher culture demands that the language which represents a higher culture should have its right. We German Balts look back with grief upon the times when too-hard [conditions] hampered the melting together of the tribes (Estonian, Latvian and German peoples) . . . But grief for the past should not weaken us for the present; it should double our strength to finish the work of peace, even though late. To elevate and spread education among our people—that is the greatest task which rests upon every thinking Balt, whichever of the three tribes he may belong to. Education itself may be named as desired, it may be written in German, Latvian, Estonian, Russian, or French letters, we do not ask its name but what it is . . . If today the Russian or Estonian culture stood above the German, we would become Russian or Estonian with no more effort than the rich require to become poor.[39]

But, in conclusion, the author writes that since the German culture is the dominant, the highest, there is no sense in lowering the cultural level of the Estonians by limiting them to the use of the Estonian laguage. It is no crime for an Estonian to absorb the German culture, since it gives him the means of higher education. It is not the mother-tongue of the child which is important and decisive in his educational and cultural progress, but the language in which he got his education—German. Therefore the Estonian language, because of the small number of the people, can never create such a culture as that of Germany, and will never present such attraction.

And though in principle the author does not oppose Estonian or Latvian higher education:

It would be a waste of material and educational forces if we should undertake seriously to have higher education done in the Latvian or Estonian languages, generally or in individual schools. When one thinks of this principal carried through in all our schools, one has to admit that it would be equivalent to the ruin of our entire educational system. From this . . . point of view we hold such a desire to the harm of our country. . . . Where the languages of peoples are not alike, the language of science is.[40]

It is the higher language (German) which should be applied.

Were it conceivable for us that Latvians or Estonians could once swing . . . to a full cultural ability in an original manner and language, to a culture of their own equal to the German or Russian, could reach an independent nationality, we should co-operate with joy to the attainment of this goal. But since this goal is unattainable according to human foresight, we do not reach for it, and though we can understand such a desire on the part of others, we cannot approve it.[41]

From such a statement we can see the real attitude of the so-called liberals. In their liberalism was the feeling of German cultural superiority and the hidden hope that the intelligent Estonian would ultimately choose voluntary Germanization.

Others believed in the complete futility of the Estonians' striving toward higher education. "It is an idle dream" writes one liberal.[42] He develops the theory that a people like the Estonians or Latvians could not because of their small number and poor economy, develop a high culture. The most they could achieve would be one university. The academic level of such an institution would necessarily be inferior.

The author believes the Germanization of Estonia to be a matter of the future. He points out the tendency of some well-to-do farmers to use the German language, but adds that these are only sporadic occurrences. He continues:

On the other hand, one asks how far this movement [towards the exclusive use of Estonian in cultural circles] could go with time, and although the idea of an Estonianization of the provinces, reaching through all social strata, is to be admitted as a possibility, even though only remote, . . . despite its undeniable vitality in the present, it is difficult to assume that it [the Estonian language] should at all be considered to be something other than a peasant language . . . Only a great nation will produce that abundance of spiritual productions which an unbroken chain of cultural progress from generation to generation is capable of producing, while linguistically isolated small peoples— even if they have for a long time played an outstanding role in world history, either through special native ability or as a result of extraordinary good fortune—moral stagnation and impoverishment must necessarily step in once again . . . Such a small nation will be able to bear the expenses of a cultural language [Kultursprache] of its own only with difficulty.[43]

The real issue, in our author's opinion, between the Baltic Germans and the Estonians is not the national differences —since the wealthy Estonians are becoming Germanized—but the social difference between the German landlord and the Estonian peasant. The author expresses his conviction that with the progressing emancipation of Estonia, a healthy economic foundation, and the creation of landowning Estonian peasantry, the process of Germanization will occur by itself.

The Estonian intelligentsia was aware of some weaknesses of cultural growth—in the villages, for example. As long as cultured and educated Estonians did not wish to return to the village, there was a danger that the countryside would lag culturally behind the city.

Voldemar Jannsen early saw that the future of the Estonian people depended upon the economic and cultural progress of the peasant, who, he rightly contended, was the backbone of the people. That is why he dedicated so much energy toward the creation and spread of agricultural societies. This theory was also stressed by many Germans. In their liberal publication, the *Baltische Monatsschrift,* the Germans wrote that, if the Estonians wished to maintain their nationality, they had to realize that only the wealthier peasants would be able to rally the poorer and the landless peasants. They contended that only the peasant who achieved his wealth by hard work would attain self respect. Thus admiration and imitation on the part of the poorer peasants would lead to the universal development of a strong, confident personality. Such ideas, expressed by Germans and greatly taken over by Estonian intellectuals, led to the development of an Estonian national ideology which lasted until the first revolution of 1905.

CHAPTER VIII

Russification and the Decline of Militant Estonian Nationalism

1. Russification and German Reaction

After the initiation of the Russification policy of Alexander III a sharp struggle between the German Lutheran and the Russian Orthodox churches developed in the Baltic provinces.[1] As long as the Lutheran Church had complete freedom of action without the interference of the Russian government and the Russian Church, it showed little interest in the cultivation of Estonian nationalism. Beginning with the second half of the nineteenth century the Lutheran Church stressed in all its utterances the superiority of German culture and professed the hope that with the emancipation and the growth of the intelligentsia the Estonians would become Germanized and finally feel and think as Germans. The German clergy did not oppose the development of the Estonian language, since they realized the usefulness of the language among the peasants, and since they had no fear of loosing their cultural domination in Estonia. Nevertheless, for the German Balts the cultural growth of the Estonian nation—if it had to grow—meant its Germanization.

Since emancipation resulted in the growing economic independence of the peasantry, the demand for education grew steadily. In the 'eighties and 'nineties a strong city popula-

111

tion developed, making Tartu, Pärnu, and Narva cities with Estonian majorities. More and more Estonians went to school, and many also entered and graduated from Tartu University. A new Estonian professional class developed and grew steadily. During this period the Russification of the University and of the school system endangered the German cultural monopoly in the Baltic provinces.

There developed a struggle between the German Balts and the Russian Government for the cultural and political dominance of the Baltic provinces. As the Estonians grew in economic and cultural stature, their demands for freedom from the overprotection of the Germans grew louder. In the light of the changed situation, the Baltic nobility and the German clergy adopted new tactics. They began limited support of the national aspirations of the Estonians as the lesser of the two evils—the alternative being Russification. Therefore, when the Russian government tried to organize govermental schools in the cities and larger villiages, where the Russian language would dominate, the German pastors warned the people of the danger of Russification.[2] The pastors tried thus to become the heralds of Estonian nationalism. They staunchly supported the continuation of religious schools with the Estonian language used in all subjects. Such a policy, they felt assured, would keep the peasants good Lutherans, and protect them from the blandishments of the Orthodox Church. During the years 1900 to 1905, the pastors, including many Estonians by this time, endeavored to make Estonian nationalism and Protestantism appear synonymous. They stressed the Russian elements of the Orthodox Church—to become an Orthodox Church member was tantamout to losing Estonian nationality and becoming Russian; to be a Lutheran was to remain an Estonian.

Despite the new-found concern of the clergy for the cultural welfare and independence of the Estonians, there obviously remained unsolved issues.

It was not easy for the German pastors to conceal their

real interests in going along with the growing Estonian nationalism. There were issues in which the Estonian temper did not coincide with that of the German Balts, especially the question of the privileges of the German landlords and the *Ritterschaften,* obviously strongly resented by the entire Estonian population. The struggle for Estonian loyalty was reflected in the Estonian press, which, in the case of the publications, remained hostile to the German pastors. It was clear to Estonians that, though Germans and Russians tried equally to win them, neither wished to see full Estonian emancipation. The history of the Estonian press clearly reflects how the Russian government checked its development. Of twenty-nine Estonian newspapers and periodicals in existence during the 'eighties and 'nineties, only sixteen were left by 1904; the rest had been forbidden. When Jakob Kõrv, the editor of the Tallinn newspaper *Valgus,* wished to expand his newspaper into a daily, he was refused permission. When K. A. Hermann attempted to publish in Tartu a thrice-weekly periodical called *Sõnumeid* (News), he was refused. The request of the editor of *Eesti Postimees* to enlarge his weekly into a daily was rejected by the authorities. This showed how much the Russian government feared the growth of Estonian national spirit. It was determined to stop it by any means.

2. The Decline of Estonian Nationalism

The steady pressure of the Russian government upon the Baltic provinces hampered cultural growth. It also put the social activities of the Estonians into a strait-jacket. The suppression of political activities during the period of Russification brought about a strong anti-alcoholic movement in Estonia. Since this was the only form of mass-organization not forbidden by the Russian government, it consolidated Estonian cultural forces for the time being.[3]

The *Karskuse Sõber* (The Friend of Temperance) spread

all over the country. In every city, in every town and village, local units appeared. Under the name of fighting alcoholism, the *Karskuse Sõber* kept the Estonian spirit alive by organizing lectures on every topic, concerts, dancing-parties, and social gatherings. The pastor, poet, historian, and national leader Villem Reiman (1861-1917) became the heart and soul of the organization.

Reiman belonged to the new generation of Estonian intellectuals. A graduate of Tartu University (1887), he was one of the organizers of the *Karskuse Sõber*. He had also taken part in organizing the *Eesti Üliõpilaste Selts* (Estonian Student Society) in 1883.[4] Under the influence of Jakob Hurt, Reiman became interested in Finno-Ugric linguistics, and, later, in Estonian history. He was one of the first educated Estonians to use the Estonian language in his home. The fact that this practice was regarded by most intellectuals as a symbol of backwardness indicates how strong the influence of the German culture remained as late as the 1880's and '90's.[5] He became one of the first few pastors who connected the Christian religion with the Estonian national spirit; throughtout his life he cared for the economic and spiritual needs of his people.[6] Reiman was active in the Estonian Learned Society, and wrote articles for the *Postimees*. Because of his anti-Russian activities, he was often subject to pressures and even house-arrests.

During the second half of the nineteenth century, Tartu grew in importance as the center of Estonian nationalism. This was due to several factors, such as: better economic conditions favoring the growth of a stronger peasantry; also Tartu University attracted increasing numbers of students; the Estonian press and literature centered there. Under the pressures of Russification a new generation grew up, imbued with the ideas of Jannsen, Hurt and Jakobson. By his own example a great interest toward the past and present Estonian culture, Reiman fostered such an interest among the young students.

Together with Reiman, another Estonian pastor greatly influenced the minds of the intelligentsia. He was Johann Kõpp (1874-195?). A graduate of the theology department of Tartu University in 1906, he became a leading personality in the Estonian Student Society, three times its president. Kõpp was active in the revival of religious life. In his speeches and publications, he tried to establish popular acceptance of the Lutheran Church. He strongly opposed the church as practised in the Baltic provices. His aim was to make religion an organic part of Estonian life, and the Lutheran church a people's church. Since many Estonians still considered the Lutheran church as a German institution, it was not an easy task for Kõpp to destroy this age-old suspicion.[7] Both Reiman and Kõpp, through the Estonian Student Society and in their capacities as pastors, continued the work of Jannsen. Both men had deep religious convictions, but neither shared Jannsen's pro-German attitude. Reiman and Kõpp belonged to the new generation, which continued to strengthen Estonian national consciousness through religion, by separating it from its German origin.

3. The Continuation of Russification

As the pressure from below against the dominance of the Germans in the Baltic provinces grew stronger in the form of organized Estonian and Latvian nationalism, the German position was threatened even more sharply from above by the continued campaign of the Russifiers.[8] What Samarin and Katkov could not achieve in the Baltic provinces, another follower of the Slavophile idea continued. He was a Russian senator, Nikolai Manassein (1835-1895), who was active during the reigns of Alexander II and Alexander III in behalf of the Latvians and Estonians. Acting on a complaint by the Baltic nobility against governor Uexküll Güldenband for his liberal attitude toward the growing nationalism of the Latvians and Estonians, Tsar Alexander III appointed Manassein to check conditions on the spot. Manassein received thousands of complaints and proposals from Estonians and Latvians. In his report to the Tsar, the investigator sharply criticized the Baltic nobles' abuses of the Latvians and Estonians. He demanded that schools be freed from the supervision and dominance of the Germans, that church supervision be taken from the Germans and given to the people, and the nobles forfeit their judicial and other privileges.[9] Manassein's report evoked a loud protest from the German nobility. The Russian government took action, however, not to improve conditions among the Estonians and Latvians, but to facilitate Russification during the following decades.[10]

In 1888 the Russian government abolished the right of the German nobles to maintain their own police force. In 1889 followed a new court-order in which the nobles lost an additional part of their control over the Estonian and Latvian population: justices of the peace, previously appointed by the nobles, became appointees of the Russian administration. The Russian language was introduced into all govermental offices to replace German.[11]

M. Kapustin, curator of schools in Estonia and Livonia, exerted a strong pressure for cultural Russification. Under his jurisdiction were all elementary and high schools, and also the Tartu University. Wherever he could he introduced the Russian language, also replacing German professors with Russians. In 1887 Russian became the only language of instruction permitted. The Russian government tried to replace communal and parochial schools, where the German pastors had control, with schools supported and controlled by the Ministry of Education. Even in private schools, the Russian language was enforced as the language of instruction. This resulted in the closing of many private schools, since there were not enough teachers and pupils who could use the language. The forceful Russification resulted in the ruin of education rather than its improvement. The existence of Estonian schools was in peril. The heaviest blow against German cultural dominance was given with the Russification of Tartu University. As a result many German professors and students left the University.[12] The University fell under ministerial control in 1889; Russification, however, had begun as early as 1885.

The change at Tartu University was without significance for the cultural development of the people as a whole, since there were few Estonian students attending the University prior to 1890. In a limited sense the University had an influence upon its few Estonian students. Most of the Russian students were imbued with liberal and revolutionary ideas, which they easily transmitted to their Estonian fellows. At first the Estonian student radicals, who stood staunchly against everything that was German, were friendly toward the policy of the Tsar. Soon, however, they realized the hopelessness of expecting help from the Tsar against the nobles. This realization came during the following years, when it became obvious to the Estonian intelligentsia that the government in St. Petersburg was no friend of Estonian culture, as it became evident in the Alexander School question. After twenty-five years the question of the much-publicized Alexander School was finally settled. Instead of the Alexander School, the Russian government created in 1888 with the collected money a Russian school near Poltsamaa. The Estonian Literary Society, which had lost much of its fervor during the preceeding years, was closed by the Russian government in 1893.

While Russification was on its move, an economic crisis hit southern Estonia, where the national movement was strongest. Economic distress and Russification stopped the national renaissance from growing and brought it into stagnation, hopelessness, and passivity.

Some support for Russification rose to the surface from among Estonian intellectuals. Jakob Kõrv (1849-1896) became a supporter of the Russification policy. A man of varied intellectual interests, he was for a time an elementary school teacher, then attended Tartu University. He became inter-

ested in educational problems, philosophy, and ultimately,
ın the Finnish language.

Kõrv was early influenced by Carl Robert Jakobson, and
he wrote for Jakobson's *Sakala*. In 1882 Kõrv bought a newspaper, the *Valgus* (Light), which he published in Tallinn.
In his newspaper he strongly supported the policies of the
Russian government.[13] Kõrv attacked the Estonian press, particularly the *Virulane* (the Vironian) and its editor, Jaak
Järv (1852-1920). Järv, a former pupil of Jakobson and con-
tributor to the *Sakala,* had become an able and successful
editor and publisher, starting in 1882 in Tallinn his own
newspaper, the *Virulane*. He continued in the anti-German
tradition of Jakobson; at the same time he did not share Jakobson's optimism in hoping for help in behalf of the Estonian cause from the Russian government. Järv also strongly
defended the interests of the working class, which made him
popular among the latter. Though he did not criticize the
Russian government (a fact for which many Estonians accused him of advocating Russification), he was attacked by
Kõrv's *Valgus* for disloyalty to the regime. As a result of
Kõrv's intrigues, Järv was deported by the Russian authorities and his newspaper closed; thus the battle between the
Valgus and the *Virulane* ended.[14]

Generally the period 1880 to 1900 can be characterized as
the low point of the Estonian press. The death of Jakobson
and economic distress, combined with the increasing pressure
of the Russian government, brought to light weak spots in
the Estonian intelligentsia. The subserviency of Kõrv to the
Russian government was not the only sign of Estonian moral
decadence. Another figure, Ado Grenzstein (1849-1916) was
even more open in his pro-Russian policy, and, because of
his greater intellectual abilities, did more harm to the cause
of Estonian nationalism.

Grenzstein studied in Germany, Austria and St. Petersburg. Returning home in 1881, he tried to become a contrib-
utor to Jakobson's *Sakala;* being refused, he began to work

instead for the pro-German *Eesti Postimees* (The Mailman). In 1882 Grenzstein began to publish his own newspaper, the *Olevik* (The Present). He did not intend to leap into political controversy; what he had in mind was to educate and enlighten the people. But the time did not allow him to adhere to his purpose. He entered into controversy over the privileges of the Baltic nobility, and, though in a more conciliatory way than Jakobson, he sought their abolition.[15]

In his book *Herrenkirche oder Volkskirche-Eine estnische Stimme im baltischen Chor,* Grenzstein made his strongest attack upon the German nobility. He analyzed the domination of the Baltic provinces by the Germans and the share of the German Lutheran Church in this domination. Grenzstein showed how very little had been done by the Lutheran church to make Christianity a part of the cultural heritage of the Estonian people. Thanks to its own behavior the Lutheran church had provided a deep cleavage between the Estonian people and itself, thus creating two separate religious communities—the *Herrenkirche* (Church of lords) and the *Volkskirche* (Church of the people). Grenzstein compared the Baltic Church *(Herrenkirche)* with the Ultramontane Catholics. While professing brotherly love as enjoined in the Christian religion, the *Herrenkirche* actually lived from the hard labor of the Estonian people.[16] Grenzstein's book was only, however, one stepping-stone in his political metamorphosis.

With Carl Jakobson's death, however, and the weakening of the *Sakala*, Grenzstein's *Olevik* became the best Estonian newspaper. By its contents and language it was a newspaper for the educated and the well-to-do. It was nationalistic, but far from being radical. Until 1888 Grenzstein continued along nationalistic lines. During the early stages of the struggle between the German Balts and the Russian government, he remained neutral. After 1890, however, he radically changed his position, and with the years he completely deserted the cause of his people, becoming a strong supporter of Russification. During this period of change most of his co-workers left his *Olevik* and went over to the *Postimees,* which, under the editorship of Karl A. Hermann, became the only nationalistic Estonian newspaper. Despite his support of the Russian government, Grenzstein could never get the complete confidence of the Russian authorities, as Kõrv did. Nor did Grenzstein completely desert the interests of his people. He became active in the anti-alcohol movement, helping organize affiliations of the *Karskuse Sõber* society in every little town. Thus Grenzstein, despite his renegade ideas, helped in another way to preserve the Estonian national spirit, though he did it without nationalistic intentions. We can see how far he went in his pro-Russian attitude: in his *Olevik* he thanked the Russian government for the closing of the Estonian Literary Society in 1893. It seems that he completely lost his belief in the vitality of small nations. Grenzstein saw in the final cultural and political merger of the Baltic provinces and Russia the best and only historical solution for the Estonian people.[17]

As mentioned before, the only newspaper which continued to defend the Estonian national ideology (as expressed by Jannsen, Jakobson and Hurt) was, after Grenzstein's defection, the *Postimees,* which was the continuation of the *Eesti Postimees* after it had become a daily in 1891. Karl August Hermann, its owner and editor, was non-political by nature; but, as in the case of Grenzstein, the times did not let him remain aloof from the political struggle of the 1890's. Hermann tried to survive Rusification by not opposing it openly, and in his views he kept a position somewhat in between that of Grenzstein and Kõrv on one hand and that of Järv on the other.[18] Though he was far from being consistent, he managed to concentrate around his *Postimees* the best of Estonian literary forces. Despite his frequent opportunism, Hermann did much to further the growth of Estonian culture and preserve the idea of nationalism during the stormy years of Russification.

Thus it can be noted that the Russification policy of the Russian government, although it openly attacked the privileges of the Baltic nobility, making some of the Estonian intellectual leaders believe in the possibility of developing Estonian education and press without the interference by the Russian government, failed completely. It resulted however, in bringing Estonian cultural and social life to its lowest level, and to a decline in the growth of Estonian national consciousness.

CHAPTER IX

The Eve of the Revolution

1. Tõnisson and the National Liberal Party

During the 'nineties a new group of intelligentsia formed which was not content with the position of Ado Grenzstein and Karl Hermann. In 1896 this group of writers and journalists, headed by Villem Reiman, Oskar Kallas and Heinrich Koppel, purchased the *Postimees*.[1] A young lawyer, Jaan Tõnisson, was made editor and the *Postimees* became the new center of the intelligentsia in Tartu.

Tõnisson's ideology was based on the conservative nationalism of Jannsen. In the wealthy Estonian peasant he saw the core of the people and the national, political and economic strength of its future. Tõnisson did much to foster agrarian conditions advocating modern agricultural methods among the Estonian peasants. Though he wished to avoid an open clash with the Germans, their privileged position was diametrically opposed to his ideology. Much, if not most of the fertile soil still belonged to the Germans. Also city administration and the law were still in the hands of the German burghers. Tõnisson hoped to push the Germans out of their superior economic and political positions by the growing economic strength and national consciousness of the people. His appeal to Estonian national consciousness and his frequent appeals to the Germans for equal rights in the city council of Tartu were met by the latter with criticism and hatred. At the same time Tõnisson fought Russification as much as censorship would allow. Always, however, he stressed his loyalty toward the Russian government.

While fighting for the interest of the Estonian middle class and the wealthier peasants, Tõnisson neglected the interests of the landless peasants and of the workers. During the 'seventies and 'eighties these groups had had no influence in public life, and little contact with their intelligentsia. For a time Estonian lower classes were little noticed by the Estonian national leaders. At the end of the century, however, the historic scene changed greatly.

2. Conditions in the Countryside and in the Cities

At the beginning of the twentieth century conditions were relatively better than fifty years earlier. Nevertheless, the peasants were still far from being satisfied and the majority did not own their own land. Especially grave were the economic and social conditions of the poorer peasants. Their economic burden was greater than they could bear. Legally they were just as helpless as before, since the administration of their villages lay in the hands of the German nobles, the great land-owners. The situation of the peasants was even worse. Bad working conditions, no social rights, low wages, no hopes for improvement or change—this was their fate.[2]

Such conditions made the country ripe for any kind of revolutionary ideas. When ideas of socialism and revolution were brought into the country by revolutionary propagandists from Russia, the landless peasants were easily infected with unrest and with hope for a better future in the event of a revolution.

During the 1890's industrialization advanced in the cities. In Tallinn, Narva, Tartu, Viljandi and in smaller cities a proletariat developed.[3] Class-differentiation increased with the growth of the factories. The migration of the landless peasants into the cities speeded this process. Marxist ideas entered Estonia through translations from the German and many inflammatory pamphlets were published. In their early stages of activity the Estonian, Latvian and Russian workers had not thought of defying the government. Their propaganda was limited and their actions aimed toward the improvement of working conditions.

With the spread of revolutionary ideas in the Baltic provinces the Estonian workers became also more conscious of the political situation in Russia proper and on the eve of the twentieth century became more hostile to the Tsarist regime.

Of no small influence were the Estonian craftsmen working in Germany, who came back home and spread the ideas of Socialism among their fellow-Estonians. Also of importance were some German Social-Democratic newspapers, such as the *Leipziger Volkszeitung,* which could be bought in Tartu in 1896. Much illegal literature was brought from Germany, and it did a thorough job of spreading socialistic ideas among the workers and intelligentsia.[4]

The growing revolutionary movement in Russia and the many Russian students who came to study at Tartu University formed another channel through which socialistic, liberal and revolutionary ideas entered Estonia. Owing to strict political supervision, however, no socialistic party could be organized before the beginning of the twentieth century. Although Tartu became the center of Estonian intelligentsia, the heart of revolutionary movements became Tallinn, a growing industrial and port city where about seventy per cent of the 75,000 inhabitants were Estonians, and where the greatest number of workers were concentrated. The political and cultural life in Tallinn was dominated by German society. One corporation with headquarters in the city was the *Ritterschaft und Landschaft,* representative body of the so-called knights, one of the few remaining pure feudal local administrations in Europe. Another citadel of German privilege was the city council, with its over-representation of the German burghers. The Estonian city element consisted mainly of workers, craftsmen, servants and minor governmental workers.

3. Päts and the Radical Nationalists

At the beginning of the twentieth century many Estonian intellectuals—lawyers, doctors, teachers—moved into Tallinn. They spoke Estonian and did not wish to join German or Russian society. They formed their own social groups, organizing societies under such innocent-sounding names as the Cycling Society, since the Russian administration was suspicious of any Estonian organized group. This new circle needed its own voice which the *Teataja* became.[5]

Because of strict censorship, the *Teataja* did not call itself socialist, nor did it openly promote revolutionary ideas. It appealed to the workers of Tallinn, urging them to demand better working conditions, and it concentrated around itself many of the intelligentsia who were not satisfied with the policy of Tõnisson and the *Postimees*. From the revolutionary ideas which were gaining currency and from the articles of the *Teataja*, the workers realized that their own economic interests were different from those of the Estonian middle classes.

The editor of the *Teataja* was Konstantin Päts (1874-1941). He belonged to the Russian Orthodox Church of his parents; his mother was of Russian descent. After graduating from school he went to study in the Russian Orthodox seminary in Riga in which his older brother was enrolled. Both brothers studied in the seminary since it was free, including room and board. This seminary was intended by the Russian government for the Russification of the Estonian population. But, despite official intentions, Konstantin Päts as well as many other Estonians developed strong nationalistic feelings while studying there. Thus the seminary acually fostered the national awakening of the Estonian intelligentsia despite the original intention of the Russian government to make the seminary a tool for their Russification policy. At that time the seminary was the only institution of advanced education where the Estonian and Latvian languages were taught. The language courses became unintended lessons in national awakening. The young students from the provinces became more and more interested in their people, and those interests overshadowed their religious aims. They read much, and, since their libraries did not offer them enough reading material, they organized their own underground library.[6] From this library Päts gained an interest in the philosophy of Proudhon, which influenced his early social thinking.

After getting his Gymnasium diploma in Pärnu, Päts studied Law at Tartu University. During those years (the nineties), the University was already Russified, and it had many students from the interior Provinces of Russia, as well as from Poland and the Caucasus. Nevertheless, the German student corporations still dominated cultural and student life in Tartu. Päts was refused admission to the Estonian Student Society because he belonged to the Russian Orthodox Church. He and several other Estonian students who did not share the general pro-German attitude of the Society tried to organize their own organizations, but did not receive permission. For lack of other outlets, Päts, Jüri Jaakson (the future director of the Estonian State Bank), and others went lecturing in such outside societies as the *Karskuse Sõber* and *Vanemuine,* thereby keeping contact with the Estonian people. The nationalist and liberal Estonian students were in close contact with the many liberal-minded Russian professors and with Russian, Polish, and Caucasian students, among whom there circulated revolutionary ideas. This was in contrast to the Estonian Student Society, which kept away from political activities, standing aloof from the interests of the people and their growing nationalism.[7]

Meanwhile the government's policy of Russification had increased the conservatism of the Baltic Germans. The pressure of the Russian administration upon Baltic institutions brought the attention of the Baltic nobility to their own affairs and narrowed their horizon at a time when they needed an understanding of the revival within the Estonian people. At the decisive moment, it diminished their ability to act and their readiness to try to give a direction to the Estonian and Latvian awakening which would be agreeable to German Baltic interests. The conservatism of the Baltic Germans aided (in a negative way) the Russification of some of the Estonian intelligentsia, or at least their temporary abandonment of political activism. At first there was a spirit of disillusionment with politics, and many leaders believed it better for the Estonian people to stay away from politics and concentrate all their energy on cultural work. "Do not touch politics, it will destroy you,"—appealed Jakob Hurt to the Estonian Student Society in 1892.[8] For a time the society followed this advice. The same spirit dominated the *Postimees* in Tartu, under the leadership of Jaan Tõnisson and leader of the anti-alcohol movement, Villem Reiman. Jannsen's slogan "The Tsar, religion and the fatherland" became now *Seaduslikkus, kõlblus, rahvus* ("legality, morality, nationalism").

During the closing decades of the nineteenth century one of Hegel's ideas was widely accepted—namely, that the most important action was to lead the people towards moral emancipation. According to Hegel's philosophy, the development of national consciousness was the highest level of a peoples' economic and cultural development. Thus leading intellectuals believed that the foundation of the emancipation of the Estonian people lay in the growth of the national consciousness of the peasant—the bulk and body of the people.[9] National spirit had reached the educated classes first; therefore, it was natural that the intelligentsia profited most from such a theory. The Estonian intelligentsia of Tartu was the leading body of this philosophy, represented by Jannsen, and later Hurt and Reiman. There the awakening of the people started at the top, among the Estonian intelligentsia, and went downwards, to the Estonian workers and peasants.

Things were different in Tallinn, where there was no Estonian intelligentsia, but only the leaderless masses. For those hard-working servants, craftsmen, and workers, the highly idealistic Hegelian philosophy had no appeal. "The slave has no nationality," Päts said in his *Teataja*, and he began his work from a different angle. Päts saw the issue as economic. To him, difficult living conditions were sterile ground for the national idea.[10] The *Postimees* saw in such ideas socialistic and Marxistic theories that came from revolutionary Russia and Social Democratic Germany. This opinion was partly true, but Päts never actually became a Marxist or socialist, as could be seen during the Revolution and the following period of independence of the Estonian Republic. He was influenced rather by Russian Economism, a school of political thought distinct from socialism and Marxism. Thus Päts and the *Teataja* engaged in political struggle, fighting for the improvement of conditions for the common man without following any specifically designed program. Ultimately there developed two distinct centers of political influences: the conservative, bourgeois-national movement under the guidance of Jaan Tõnisson was backed by a growing Estonian middle class and well-to-do peasantry and intelligentsia in Tartu; owing to the dynamic personality of Päts and the great number of Estonian workers, the other political center, more radical and revolutionary, developed in Tallinn.

4. The Campaign for the City Council of Tallinn

Päts believed in the importance of institutions; therefore, he struggled for the control of the Tallinn city government. At the turn of the century, the Estonians had control over the

village commune only. The city government was completely
in the hands of the German nobility and the German burghers. Only those who owned houses and paid a certain minimum property tax could vote. There was a growing number
of Estonian house-owners, but they were unorganized and
thus without representation in the city council of Tallinn.
The best property was in German hands. The Estonians were
mostly small house-owners, from whom little political activity
was expected. But they initiated a clever strategy against
the Germans: they, and other eligible voters within their
faction, declared members of the Estonian intelligentsia as
co-owners of their property, thus adding to the number of
eligible voters an active, self-conscious group. The Germans
warned them that intelligentsia would soon take over their
owners.

Until this time (1902), there had been no election cam-
paigns. The mayor called together the council and prepared
a list of new candidates, usually favoring the Germans. The
electors had to accept the lists. The chairman of the *Ritterschaft,* Baron von Dellinghausen, and Mayor von Hüeck
asked Bellegarde, the governor, to refuse Estonians permission to hold their political meetings freely. The Germans
feared losing control over Tallinn; they asserted that Estonian mismanagement would ruin the city. But the governor
did not listen. He granted the Estonians freedom of assembly.
Actually, Tallinn had been neglected under the management
of the Germans. The city was growing steadily, but the city
fathers had failed to provide adequate utilities, such as drinking water and electricity. Only the center, the old city, was
kept clean, since the German burghers residing there could
afford to take care of their houses and their streets. Such
was the situation when the elections came. The *Teataja* became the general headquarters of the election committee;
members were sent from house to house to teach the Estonians
how to cast their vote.[11] The results were surprising: the
Estonians and Russians together claimed 48 seats out of 60.

In order to have the support of the Russian administration, the Estonians agreed to elect as mayor a Russian official who worked in the Governmental committee for the affairs of the Estonian peasants. His name was Hiacintov, and he was known as a liberal-minded man. He had good relations with the official Russian administration, since his brother was a department director in the ministry of transport. Päts became deputy-mayor. All this exasperated the Germans, and especially von Dellinghausen, who was surprised by the cleverness of the Estonians in putting a Russian at the front of their political machine. The Germans would have preferred Päts to the hated Russian, Hiacintov, as mayor. Thus a major battle of far-reaching political significance was won in the capital of the Estonian province. It was won through the cooperation of the intelligentsia and the middle classes. It was won mainly because of the strong national consciousness of the Estonian citizens and the able leadership of Konstantin Päts.[12]

5. Economic Rivalry between the Estonian and German Middle Classes

Of great importance for the formation of a strong national spirit was the increase and cooperation of Estonian businessmen and the growth of finance. This consolidation was greatly facilitated by the leader of the Estonian middle class, Jaan Tõnisson, and his active supporters. With the rise of an Estonian majority in the cities and towns, the young Estonian middle class had to face competition with an older and stronger rival, the German burgher group. Tõnisson placed his faith in cooperatives as the backbone of a strong Estonian business and middle class.[13] With the experience of his trips to Austria and Germany, Tõnisson helped to organize a cooperative movement in Estonia. This movement, starting in 1899, soon reached a national scale. New banks came into being helping the Estonian businessman, the artisan, the craftsman, the peasant. The cooperative movement

facilitated greatly the development of the economic independence of the Estonian peasants helping them to compete
with the experiencd and wealthier Germans.

The German businessmen watched with anger and fear
the growing independence of their competitors. The rivalry
grew with the increasing success of the Estonian middle class
and the flourishing of Estonian enterprises, large and small.
On the eve of the 1905 revolution relations grew worse between the two groups. Rivalry between the German and
Estonian merchants had gone so far that both groups appealed to their respective nations for boycotts. In December,
1903, the Germans printed and circulated lists of Estonian
businessmen who should be boycotted by Germans.[14] The
Postimees did not support such actions and in an appeal to
its Estonian readers, the *Postimees* accused the German press,
particularly the *Nordlivländische Zeitung*, of fostering the
boycott. The German press, however, accused the *Postimees*
of hypocrisy: it contended that the Estonian newspaper only
waited for a better time for such action. The other Estonian
newspaper, the *Uudised* (News) remained neutral, since it
supported a third faction, the rural cooperative element,
which was struggling against both the German and Estonian
businessmen. The *Uudised* believed that the rural cooperative movement was not yet strong enough to attack openly
the positions of the rival merchants.[15] The triangle of the
German and Estonian businessmen and the cooperatives became a force in itself in fermenting nationalism and revolutionary ideas among the masses. The displacement of the
German middle class by the Estonian middle class led to
sharp antagonism between those groups. It fostered the
growth of national consciousness among the Estonian bourgeoisie and lessened the attractiveness of Germanization. The
Estonian bourgeoisie was looking for new weapons in its
struggle to maintain its economic position against the old
privileges of the Germans, and in the growing nationalism
of the masses it found its best ally. But while it was appealing

to the national sentiment of the people, backed by Jaan Tõnisson and the new Estonian bourgeois press, the rising Estonian working class developed its own class-consciousness. It had been influenced by the Marxist propaganda within its ranks, by the growth of the Latvian Social-Democratic movement, and by the revolutionary movement all over Russia.[16]

At the beginning of the twentieth century the Germans, under the fire of Russification and pressed by growing Estonian competition, began to feel very insecure. They feared being driven from the local governments by the growing Estonian majorities. The Baltic German press, however, tried to calm these fears by explaining to its readers that the Estonian national movement was only trying to eliminate the abuses of the past, and seeking equal civil rights with the Germans.[17] The *Nordlivländische Zeitung* even published an open address by Jaan Tõnisson stressing the willingness of the Estonian people to cooperate with the Germans, but not to be dominated by them. Tõnisson wrote:

> This appears possible only on the basis of a healthy reciprocity, in no case however under the past assumptions, according to which the German element, despite its minority in the city and country, exercised exclusive domination while the overwhelming majority of the population, (without rights) had to remain in paralysing passivity under the fulfillment of difficult duties.[18]

The young Estonian middle class did not wish to challenge the Germans to an open fight—therefore, the conciliatory tone of Tõnisson. The point was that Tõnisson, and with him the majority of the liberal-national party, believed in evolution as a result of economic emancipation. They hoped thus to gain victory without bloodshed and boycotts. At the same time, the liberals stressed in their press the nationalistic nature of their struggle against the German middle class and nobility, in such a way making their economic struggle an appeal to the national feelings of the Estonian peasants as well as the workers and intelligentsia.

The *Postimees* analyzed the possibilities of a compromise with the Germans, and came to the conclusion that, as long as German leadership was against the natural development of affairs in Estonia, there could be no compromise. Tõnisson ad his National Liberal Party hoped that the economic and cultural growth of the Estonian people would force the Baltic Germans to accept the former's aspirations and agree upon the political and economic as well as cultural equality of both. Not all, however, among the supporters of Tõnisson shared the latter's optimistic views. At the same time the liberal German Balts feared that with the acquisition of political equality, the Estonian people would ultimately displace them from their economic and political superiority, and, being a minority, the German Balts would be a helpless object of reprisal by the Estonian people.

The fears of the Germans were well founded, as were the suspicions of the Estonian bourgeois. The events of the 1905 revolution in the Baltic provinces proved it most convincingly.

CHAPTER X *

The 1905 Revolution

1. The Eve of the Revolution

The decade preceding the 1905 revolution found the Estonians seething with unrest. Despite the land reforms and the abolition of many of the privileges of the nobles, the conditions of the peasants remained bad and often hopeless. More than seventy-five per cent of them did not own their land; taxes were high and dependence upon the landlord was still great. The only contented Estonians were the well-to-do peasants who managed through very hard work and many favorable circumstances to pay all their debts to the German landlords, and become completely independent. On the bottom of the economic ladder were the landless peasants and workers. The spread of revolutionary sentiments in Russia and the collapse of Russian military might during the Russo-Japanese War aroused response among Estonians. Reactions varied according to different political groups. The Nationalist-Liberal *Postimees,* with Jaan Tõnisson as its leader, opposed any revolutionary propaganda among the Estonian people.[1] The *Teataja,* edited by the radical Konstantin Päts, did not support the revolutionary movement openly because of censorship, but it spread revolutionary ideas among its readers—made up mainly of the intelligentsia and workers of Tallin—by criticising working conditions

135

throughout the country. It enlightened the workers about their rights, attacked the German privileges and demanded equality of the Estonians with the German Balts. Päts saw in the economic factor the major force which shaped the society but he accepted the importance of the national issue, at the same time appealing to the economic interest of the workers and landless peasants. While the *Postimees* steered clear of Russian political developments, the *Teataja* felt that the Russian revolutionary parties had much in common with the Estonian people in their fight for their rights. Päts believed that his people could achieve political independence only with the help of the Russian revolutionary movement. Thus there developd a bitter quarrel between the *Postimees* and the *Teataja*. In Tartu the socialistic newspaper *Uudised* (News) almost openly spread revolutionary ideas among the Tartu intelligentsia, the workers and landless peasants of the surrounding area. It was edited by an educated and able revolutionary, Peter Speek, who acquired his revolutionary background and experience while living in St. Petersburg. The *Uudised* described conditions in Estonia and compared them with conditions in Western Europe, appealing to the workers to demand and fight for their rights.[2]

When the political foundations of the Russian empire began to shake during the mass strikes, the nationalist-liberal group, headed by Tõnisson opposed Estonian participation in the all-Russian revolutionary movement, he acted in behalf of the people when he felt that the time was right.[3] On April 6, 1904, the *Postimees* published the following formal demands of Russia:

[I Education]

[The public schools]

Discontinuation of forced Russification in the public schools. Public schools must serve the enlightenment and education of the Estonian people. In all public, private, and parochial grade schools the Estonian language must become the mother tongue.

In all grade schools the Russian language must become a required subject in all grades.

The schools must be supported by the state, by local self-government, or by the city-council.

Grade school must be free and obligatory for all children, except in the parochial schools, where it would be free but not obligatory.

The inspection and control of the grade schools should be under the supervision of the local communities, but not under the sole control of the governmental inspector, who would abuse the freedom of teaching in the schools according to his political views.

There should be organized teacher-seminaries for the preparation of qualified school-teachers.

[The parochial and city schools]

The language of instruction in the second grade level should be Estonian.

[The high school]

In the middle-schools [Gymnasiums, vocational Gymnasiums, and commerce Gymnasiums] the Estonian language of instruction of the pupils of Estonian origin, which should be obligatory.

[The universities]

There should be a regular professorship, as well as lectureship, for the Estonian language at Tartu University.

In the theological department the future pastors who will work in Estonian communities should study in the Estonian language.

The University should approach the Estonian people by offering courses and lectures in the Estonian language in order to raise the cultural and educational standard of the people.

[Professional education]

For each province [Estonia and Livonia] there should be built at least one agricultural school; for each country, at least one lower agricultural school; the language of instruction should be Estonian.

For the fostering of agricultural knowledge courses should be offered for the people at those schools; they should be given in the Estonian language.

*   *   *

The 100,000 rubles collected by the Estonian people for the Alexander School should be used not for continuing the Russian city-school, but to organize an agricultural high school with Estonian as the language of instruction. The teaching plans should be drawn by the Estonian agriculural societies.

[Freedoms of education
or
Educational Rights]

Every child has the right, independent of race, religion, class or sex to enter any higher education school.

There should be given freedom to the parents to organize their children's education in their homes. [Many private tutors of Estonian as well as German origin were punished by the government if found teaching in their private homes without supervision of the city inspectors.]

The opening of private Estonian high schools should be permitted.

[II. Self-government]

Equal opportunity for all groups in Estonia to self-government. As a beginning there should be elected in the countryside a self-government representing all classes, in the cities, a city government. The next governing organization should be the county government, the highest, the *Landes-Verwaltung*, (provincial government) in which representatives from the country as well as from the cities should sit together. The Estonian counties should be united into one unit. The historic and geographic borders should be changed. The representatives from the countryside and from the cities should have equal voting rights in the provincial government. The language of the provincial government should be the local language [Estonian].

There should be a strict limit for the rights of the Russian governmental administration, and there should be separation of powers between the provincial, city, and governmental administrations.

The local police should be under the jurisdiction of the local government.

For the improvement of health the government should provide for adequate medical treatment.

[III. The courts]

The local communities in the villages should have the rights to elect their court officials.

In all the courts the language should be Estonian.

In higher courts there must be members of the courts who know Estonian.

Trial by jury should be introduced in Estonia.

[IV. Taxes]

Every citizen should pay taxes according to his income and property hence the higher the income the higher the percentage of taxes [progressive income tax.]

[V. Privileges]

Abolition of all privileges—all citizens equal before the law and the courts. Employment of civil servants should be done according to education and personal abilities, but not according to national origin or class. The rights of the women should be extended.

The privileges of the Rittergüter [Estates of the nobility], *Patronatsrecht* [the right to open stores]; the *Krugrecht*—right to keep taverns; the right to brew and sell beer; distillery-rights; [exclusive] rights on hunting, fishing, and boating; to open docks; to hold bazaars; and all similar privileges [of the nobles]— were to be abolished.

[VI. Agricultural conditions]

Land is the most important source of income; therefore, speculation in it should be limited. Those who do not have direct relations with the land should not have the right to dispose of it. The purchase of small landholdings by persons who do not make a living on the land should be forbidden.

The land of the government and church should be sold to landless peasants in units of sufficient size to support entire families.

The government should provide for the social security of all peasants in case of death, accidents, sicknesses, or old age.

[VII. Freedom of religion]

Freedom of worship and the free choice of religion must be given to everybody.

Married couples with different religious backgrounds have the right to educate their children in the religion they choose, even if one of them is an Orthodox Church member.

Freedom of religious organization within religious communities.

Introductions of the civil marriage simultaneously with the religious.

[VIII. Freedom of the person, of speech, of thought, and of organization]

No one should be kept under arrest for more than twenty-four hours without facing accusation and trial.

Freedom to join organizations, to attend meetings, to publish.

Freedom of publication in any language.

[IX. Form of the state]

Local government of each people within the Russian empire. Election of delegates from the population into the provincial government—free and without pressure.

Direct, equal and secret voting.

Elected civil servants can be recalled only through a court order before their term expires.[4]

These demands were expressed in a calm but resolute manner, which was quite a change for the heretofore moderate Tõnisson and the loyal *Postimees*. This so-called declaration of rights reflected the general feelings of the Estonian people, showing that even Tõnisson and his followers, from the middle class and the wealthy peasantry, could not afford to lose contact with the people and the times. Affairs remained in a state of suspension until the beginning of the following year.

2. Bloody Sunday and its Repercussions in Estonia

Bloody Sunday in St. Petersburg, on January 9, 1905, had its repercussions all over Estonia. Events developed with the pace of a storm in Tallinn, where the revolutionary movement was strongest among the Estonian workers. On January 12, workers from the *Dvigatel* factory went on strike. On the same day the public employees stopped working, so that there was no gas or electricity in the city. Concurrently the newspapers stopped because of a printers' strike. During the day large groups of workers demonstrated on the streets; no major disturbances ensued, however.[5] On January 14, strikes and demonstrations resulted in fights with army units.[6] On the same day in Tartu there occurred manifestations of workers and students, but without violence. Against those demonstrations the *Postimees* protested vigorously. In Pärnu striking workers demanded higher wages and an eight-hour day. Those public protests were suppressed by police and army units.[7] On January 29 even servant girls in Tallinn went on strike, demanding higher wages and better living conditions.[8]

Meanwhile, strikes among the landless peasants in the country became more and more frequent: proclamations brought from the towns into the villages helped greatly to stimulate the revolutionary fervor among them. In some villages, pitched battles occurred between peasants and the police and army; some property of German landlords was destroyed.

In the towns the youth, particularly the students of high schools and of Tartu University, stopped studying and demanded that their professors protest the Bloody Sunday in St. Petersburg.[9] While the workers and landless peasants openly defied the Russian government, the Estonian middle class stood aloof. The *Postimees* constantly appealed to the people to avoid violence.

At this early stage of the 1905 revolution all these incidents were of a spontaneous character.[10] Most actions of the workers, students, and landless peasants were not yet systematized by the revolutionary organizations of the Social Democratic or the Social Revolutionary parties, though the Social Democrats did circulate some leaflets. The governor of Estonia, Aleksei Bellegarde, satisfied some of the economic demands of the workers, such as those for shorter hours, higher wages, and the election of worker representatives to factory council. For several months the major towns were relatively quiet. With the departure of Bellegarde and the coming of a new governor, Aleksei Lopukhin, unrest and open revolt stirred once more. Lopukhin was not responsible for that unrest, however: the revolution was already on the move.

The political atmosphere all over Russia influenced the work of the city council of Tallinn. Since it was the only Estonian-dominated council, it grew in importance and became a kind of first Estonian parliament, where the people guardedly expressed their opinion. Extreme rightists and leftists among the councilmen disagreed concerning the policy to be maintained in Tallinn. The Tartu *Uudised,* now openly socialistic, sharply criticized the council in Tallinn for fostering the interests of the wealthy Estonians to the neglect of the workers and servants. At this stage of the Revolution, Konstantin Päts became less radical and opposed the socialistic Speek and the *Uudised.* He accused the socialists of being unrealistic. Answering the criticism of the socialists, he replied that it was impossible to help everybody, to provide for the poor and apply socialistic doctrines in the work of the city council—all at the very beginning of Estonia's political growth.[11]

During the year 1905, violence continued throughout the province. Strikes of the landless peasants occurred daily; hatred for the German landlords was expressed by burning of property. Hundreds of manors, with their granaries and agricultural machinery were burned during 1905. Germans were attacked and killed; tens of thousands of landless peasants refused to work, demanding higher pay. Since it was impossible for the *gendarmerie* to be everywhere at once, the German landlords were helpless. The acts of violence did not occur simultaneously all over Estonia, but sporadically, in widely separated areas. For more than a year the Germans were terrorized, often leaving their manors to look for refuge in the cities.[12]

Those revolutionary activities were inspired by the Estonian movement—the Social Democratic and the Social Revolutionary parties. Both parties worked illegally, getting their support from the city proletariat and their literature from German and Russian revolutionary circles. The many revolutionary agitators and the thousands of leaflets which they distributed had a strong influence upon the peasants, who hated the Germans and were eager to see them leave the land.[13]

Revolutionary movements often resulted in pitched battles between the Cossacks and the people. While such battles were sporadic, they contributed greatly to the growth of the revolutionary spirit, and at the same time kept the Germans fearful and ready for concessions. It can be seen from a correspondence in the *Revaler Beobachter* (The Tallinn Observer) of August 21, 1905, how frightened the German nobles became:

With increasing darkness the insecurity of the country increases frighfully. Rarely a night passes when there cannot be seen a large fire shining here or there; yes, usually there can be seen several fires simultaneously . . . As soon as a bin is filled with grain or a barn with fodder, it immediately becomes the victim of flames. The incendiaries . . . have never been caught.[14]

During the months of September and October, 1905, universal tension increased with the mounting chaos of violence in city and country. In order to maintain order and prevent looting, the Tallinn city council decided to organize a defense. They appealed for the cooperation of the workers, who agreed to participate only on the following conditions: the military patrols should be removed from the streets to avoid clashes between patrols and the defense groups; freedom of the press should be permitted; political prisoners should be liberated from the city jail. The city council agreed to the first two demands; after the approval of the governor, the workers assumed their task of patrolling the streets.

Soon, however, rumors spread among the population that the Germans were to obtain arms. This brought some protest and occasional street violence, which was, however, stifled by the worker patrols. On October 16 the workers repeated their demand for the release of political prisoners. In addition they demanded arms for the workers and 7500 rubles for aid of the factory unemployed. Upon receiving the new demands the city council agreed to all but the arming of the workers. While the council and delegates of the defense groups were holding conference, thousands of workers milled about on the streets of Tallinn. While holding an open-air meeting, the workers were attacked by army units; a terrible massacre resulted. The toll of this massacre was more than sixty dead and many more wounded.[15] The city council held an immediate meeting and reached the following resolutions: 1. It demanded that the governor punish those responsible for and those participating in the massacre. 2. It announced the discontinuation of payments to the city police. 3. It resolved to contact the various groups of citizens and organize a committee of defense. 4. It sent a telegram to the governor, accusing the army of attacking the people and praising the workers for helping to restore peace.

Meanwhile the October Manifesto of Tsar Nicholas II granting a number of concessions to the revolutionaries had become known, and the city council decided to publish it and distribute thousands of copies among the population of the city. The council added an appeal to the people to maintain peace and order. Another message was sent to the governor: it demanded that he put the police under council jurisdiction; it demanded a general amnesty for all political prisoners; it demanded the punishment of those guilty of the massacre; and finally it promised to erect a monument in Tallinn to the memory of the victims.[16]

3. October in Tartu

In Tartu activities began with a mass meeting of the students in the University Aula (Hall). A student body called *Schodka* ("meeting," in Russian) formed and demanded that the Rector discontinue classes because of the revolutionary movement in Russia. The *Schodka* demanded the acceptance of all its decisions by the *Landsmannschaften* (the union of German fraternities) and by the student council *(Studenten-Convent)*, which was the official student body representing the student corporations. The *Landsmannschaften*, however, refused to participate in the *Schodka*, since it did not want to get involved in politics.[17] On October 16, a mass meeting was held in the *Aula* with an attendance of over four thousand people—students, workers, and intelligentsia. During this meeting, revolutionary speeches were delivered by members of the Russian and Estonian Social Democratic parties. In vain, Jaan Tõnisson appealed to the group to declare their faithfulness and loyalty to the Tsar. He was pursued into the street by a number of participants, attacked, and slightly hurt. That night found crowds roaming the streets. By early morning of October 17, workers had forced the closing of all stores and shops, including the post office and all public institutions. That night saw Tartu without electricity. The first clashes occurred between the workers and the police and army. Military patrols continued to be on the streets. Tension mounted to the bursting point. Finally the news of the October Manifesto reached Tartu. Screaming and shouting against the Tsar, the people went joyfully into the streets, and expressed their joy on the occasion of the beginning of an era of freedom which the promised constitution was to bring. Sidewalk speeches were delivered; students from Tartu University and the many high schools appeared, wearing red ribbons and singing the *Marseillaise* and other revolutionary songs. Thousands of people formed a procession which marched through the streets of Tartu until it finally stopped in front of the University Aula, where again speeches were given.

On the afternoon of October 18, Jaan Tõnisson spoke in front of the city hall. He strongly appealed for calmness and common sense, but he was whistled down by the socialists, who called for the hanging of the pastors and for burning the main houses of the landowners.[18] On the next day the city was controlled by the socialists. They organized a defense group and took over from the police the maintenance of order in the city. During this day, no police were seen on the streets of Tartu. There was a steady flow of people into the *Aula,* and mass meetings were held continuously. While the workers and the radical intelligentsia openly expressed their defiance of the Tsarist regime, the *bourgeois* stood apart from the revolutionary outbursts of the people. On that same day, several Estonian societies under the leadership of Jaan Tõnisson staged a march, not with the red flag of revolution, but with their own society flags, the Russian flags, and the picture of the Tsar. This angered the revolutionary-minded people to such a degree that they attacked the procession and destroyed the Russian flags and the pictures of the Tsar. During the scuffle, Tõnisson was again attacked and hurt.

This was the end of the revolutionary days in Tartu, however. On the very next day the commanding officer of the
Russian garrison at Tartu declared that, in the event of more
violence, he was going to use force. Soon afterwards the Russian military occupied the city hall.

On the same day Tõnisson published in his *Postimees* an
appeal to the people in the name of such societies as the
Handwerkerverein (Society of Craftsmen), the *Eesti Pol-
lumeeste Selts* (Estonian Agricultural Society), the *Karskuse
Sõber* (Temperance Society), and the *Taara, Ugannia* and
Vanemuine societies. In his appeal Tõnisson declared that
the general political strike had achieved the collapse of the
autocratic regime, and that a new government would be
created. Instead of autocracy there would be a constitution.
Thus, Tõnisson contended, the goal of the strike had been
attained, and there was no necessity to continue striking and
provoking disorders.[19] On October 21 the governor declared
that the army and the police would assume control and suppress any disorder. The strikes in the town had ended, and
normal work had begun again. On that day, the editor of the
socialistic *Uudised* wrote: "A complete victory cannot be
spoken of. The proletariat must go forward and forward,
until the absolute rule of the people on a democratic basis
is achieved." [20]

4. Further Political Development

When the Latvian intelligentsia petitioned the Tsar for
more political rights and equality with the German nobles,
Estonian intellectuals were stimulated to do the same.[21]
Under the leadership of an energetic lawyer, Jaan Teemant,
a petition was sent to the Tsar in the name of the Estonian
peasants. The petition demanded political freedom, equal
voting rights with the Germans, the unification of Estonia
and northern Livonia, free and obligatory public school education; the use of the Estonian language in local institutions

and schools; their right to elect their pastors; the distribution of church and governmental lands to the peasantry; and the lowering of rents for farms.

Agrarian problems as well as self-government were stressed in the petition. Since the Tsar gave orders to record the demands of the peasants, many mistakenly believed that the lands would be distributed among them. In many localities the peasants demanded that the local authorities divide the land. When the authorities refused, the peasants, believing that the Tsar's orders were not being carried out, resorted to violence. In the face of such political upheaval the Baltic nobles granted some concessions. In the February meeting of their provincial council, they prepared a new system of representation, in which all classes would be represented. But the *Teataja* explained that even under those new provisions, only the wealthy Estonians would have a voice, while the majority of the people would be voiceless as before. Among the German nobility were some with relatively liberal views, among them Eduard von Stackelberg-Sutlem. Stackelberg and several others met some of the more conciliatory Estonian leaders unofficially, to avoid Estonian accusations of treason. Among the Estonians were Konstantin Päts, Jaan Poska, Jaan Teemant, Mihckel Pung, Georg Eduard Luiga. The radical and socialist Estonian leaders did not participate in those secret talks. To give more weight to their voice, however, the Estonian representatives asked the Germans to invite Mihkel Martna, a leading Estonian socialist. Martna demanded from the nobles general franchise in the local governments and the distribution of crown and church lands to the peasants. Martna's demands were, with the acceleration of the revolutionary unrest, supported by his more conservative fellow-Estonians. The conferences continued until the revolutionary storm brought them to an end.[22] This attempt for conciliation with the Estonian middle class was caused by the growing fear of the German nobility for the rising tide of the Revolution. Seeing no help from the Tsarist gov-

ernment against the advance of Estonian nationalism and
social unrest, they tried, in the twelfth hour, to find common
language with the Estonian bourgeoisie.[23] That the German
Balts were not ready yet to pay the full price of political and
cultural equality to the Estonians was only one cause of the
failure to reach agreement. Another cause was the growing
hostility of the Estonian masses towards the Baltic nobility,
and with the spreading of the revolution in Russia and in
the Baltic provinces, its confidence in the final victory over
Germandom, destroyed the last attempts to reach a compromise.

The revolutionary movement in Tartu was represented by
the students; but, since it was socialistic, it did not find many
followers among other groups. In Tallinn the revolutionaries
came from among the Russian civil servants and intellectuals,
whom a number of Estonian civil servants and intellectuals
joined. The Russian liberal circle had among its members
such outstanding Russian governmental workers as the lawyer Bulat, later a member of the Duma, engineer Vasnov,
factory inspector Karavanov, and many others. They met in
the Russian clubs, where political ideas, often of a revolutionary nature, were openly expressed. The group was in
contact with the Estonian intellectuals and revolutionaries.
Owing to the high standing of its members, it could and did
help greatly to promote the revolutionary movement.

Päts opposed the destructiveness of the revolutionary
masses, especially their destruction of the great German landowners. But he did not have enough power to control the
spontaneous mass movement. Especially enraging to the
peasants was the introduction of martial law. This marked
the beginning of the massacres in Tallinn, (mentioned before), which infuriated the population.[24] The influence of
the socialists grew with the excitement of the masses. Advocates of moderation lost their influence. In many towns—in
Pärnu, Valga, Viljandi, and Võru—the police were compelled
to give arms to the people.

In November of 1905 a public meeting led by Tõnisson was held in the Exhibition building in Tartu. In the name of the many Estonian societies, Tõnisson made the following opening statement:

The legal constitution, accepted by the October Manifesto, was supposed to help to bring order and law into the chaos and lawlessness under which the country suffered. Unfortunately, the people saw that the government did not have sincere intentions of introducing constitutional government. The arbitrariness of officials ruled as before. Such an attitude resulted in distrust among the people, and filled their hearts with growing restlessness. Such a situation takes the calmness from the country and pushes the people towards rebellion, which might result in general anarchy.[25]

In the name of peaceful development for the country and the people he demanded that the government exert all its power to secure constitutional government. He especially demanded freedom of conscience, speech, and the press, freedom of meeting, freedom of organization, inviolability of the person, and immediate amnesty for all political prisoners. A constitutional convention should be called, based on equal, secret and direct balloting. The convention should organize a new governmental system to secure the political rights of the people. Tõnisson demanded for the Estonian people as for all other nationalities in Russia the right of self-determination.[26]

This appeal did not result in immediate action, as the National-Liberal Party had hoped. Tõnisson's demand was the result of his losing faith in the sincerity of the Tsarist government. This shows that even the middle class, sharing though its fear of revolution felt by the Germans and the Russian government, could not defend its peaceful position any longer without losing national support.

In the cities of Tallinn, Tartu, and Pärnu revolutionary fervor brought the people out into the streets, where they openly defied the police for a time, causing bloody battles and many deaths. The Germans and the Russian administration believed that, despite the disorders, the country would remain peaceful. The day of November 28, 1905, arrived and changed the order of developments.

5. The All-Estonian Congress and the Aula Manifesto

On the 28th of November, 1905, a conference of the All-Estonian Congress was held in Tartu. Over eight hundred persons, from all parts of the country and from all political groups arrived. The meeting convened in the *Bürgermusse,* a large hall. The nominations for the executive members of the Congress went into sharp discussions and even some physical violence. The National-Liberal and the Social Revolutionary parties stood in sharp opposition. The former had its followers from among the wealthy and educated, the latter, from among the workers, landless peasants, and radical intelligentsia. The parties could not agree on matters of future policies toward the Russian government. Finally the Social Revolutionaries, headed by Peter Speek, left the *Bürgermusse*. Left without opposition, the National-Liberals elected Tõnisson as the leader of the Convention. Speek and his followers went to the *Aula,* where the radical Jaan Teemant was elected chairman of the convention.

Tõnisson and his party rejected revolutionary action; they wished to achieve complete self-government in city and country, and control over economic, educational and political development. But they wished to achieve it legally, on the basis of the October Manifesto.[27] Nevertheless, in the event of reaction by the Russian government, Tõnisson advised the Estonian people to resist passively: they should stop paying taxes, boycott the administration, and carry out other negative actions.

Those were the basic achievements of the National-Liberal party in the *Bürgermusse*. Things were quite different in the

Aula of Tartu University. The more than two hundred delegates were filled with revolutionary fervor, ready to continue the struggle for a final liberation of their country from under the yoke of the Russian government and the Baltic Germans. Among those attending were many people who had not been elected, but who nevertheless participated in the discussions and added to the fire. After heated debate and a number of revolutionary speeches, a resolution was adopted. This resolution, directed to the Russian government and the Russian people, demanded the government's resignation and called upon the Russian people to take up arms to fight against the Tsar for their freedom. The resolution concluded:

Down with the government, down with the landlords and their castles! The pastors into the bag or on the gallows! Away with the present community and school-boards! The draftees should stay home! Seize the weapons! Take whatever you can take! Do not stand idle and wait for a favor from the government! [28]

This resolution, the Aula Manifesto, was later reproduced in thousands of copies and distributed all over the country. Its effect was unexpected for conservatives and radicals alike: it not only aroused the fermenting city-population, but stimulated the peasants into action against the Russian government and the landlords.

On December 9, 1905, all factories in Tallinn stopped their work; the railway ceased operations. In the villages the peasants, especially the poor and landless, followed the instructions of the Aula Manifesto: they began to elect their own community elders, break off relations with the police and the peasant-commissars, and stop paying taxes and rent. In Tallinn and in the province of Harjumaa the government introduced martial law.[29] On December 12 the Estonian Social Democratic Party held a meeting in the *Aula* of Tartu University, where it was decided to call for a province-wide strike. The strike collapsed at the very beginning, however, owing to the lack of organization among the workers in Tartu and insufficient contact with Tallinn and other towns.[30] Meanwhile mass meetings of workers were held in the towns of Estonia, and armed workers began to move into all parts of the country. Many Latvians joined the Estonians in their punitive action against the great German landowners. The first to act on a large scale were the workers of the factories in Tallinn—they had been earlier infected by revolutionary propaganda. In the country, the landless peasants, led by revolutionaries from the towns, attacked the mansions of the landlords and burned them, often killing the owners. Many German pastors were driven away from their parishes. In many places the peasants took over the land of the nobles and divided it among themselves.

In the beginning the nobility and the Russian administration, not expecting such a rapid turn of events, failed to meet the emergency. For six days—from December 12 until December 17—there were no army units in Estonia, and the little groups of police sent from Tallinn could not be everywhere to help the nobles against the plundering workers and peasants. When army and more police units finally arrived, a country-wide repression began against the revolutionaries.[31] The Russian army and the police were aided by volunteers from the Baltic German nobility. Together they massacred the people and burned the villages killing guilty and innocent men, women, and children alike. Thus came the turning-point in the revolution, and another period of reaction and revenge.[32]

6. The Baltic Nobility at the End of the Revolution

The German *Ritterschaft* sent a declaration to Russian Premier Witte describing the revolution. The declaration stressed the guilt of the Russian government for the revolutionary movement. The *Ritterschaft* denied being the real cause of the Baltic revolution, but declared the the hostile

attitude of the government towards the German elements in
the provinces resulted in a loss of respect for the Protestant
religion and the Baltic institutions. It maintained that forced
Russification was one more mistake of the Russian government, taking away the right to use the German language
without giving Estonians the use of their own language in
the many institutions, without instituting chairs of Estonian
and Latvian in the Tartu and Riga Universities. By police
and administrative bureaucracy the Russian government had
developed only hatred against itself, which found its expression in the recent uprisings. The *Ritterschaft* did not obey the
many good objectives of the revolutionaries. They opposed
martial law as the means of pacifying the country. Necessary
measures, they held, were reform in the direction of local
self-government; the right to use the native language in all
local institutions, including the schools; permission for the
provinces to have their own provincial councils where all
provinces should be represented; and abandonment of forced
Russification.[33] Such an attitude showed a great deal of common sense and a great change in the aspirations of the Germans. Realizing that their historic role as the ruling cultural
and economic class was ended, they wished to save what could
be saved—thus the then prevailing conciliatory attitude and
the request for reforms.

The conservative Russian newspaper *Novoye Vremya*
(New Era) wrote of the Ritterschaft's declaration:

The Germans' admission that they cannot get a compromise with
the Estonians and Latvians shows a state of mind which is quite
revealing. . . . It is the first sign of a development in the political
life of the Baltic provinces. The Baltic Germans will . . . finally
be forced by the growing antagonism of the Estonians and Latvians, and by their growing force, to give way to new reforms
which will steadily weaken their positions. . . . The German
superiority has already collapsed. . . . The Germans have a false
picture of the conditions . . . and they wrongfully believe that
we [Russians] endanger their positions. . . . The danger, however, comes from a different side. . . . In local self-government

the Germans have already been chased out; they are in a minority.
. . . The Estonians are in charge of the city governments' . . .
and that is only a beginning, since their power is growing. The
time will come when we shall have to defend the weaker, this
time not the Estonians and Latvians but the Germans, since it
is our duty to defend the . . . weaker.[34]

The German fear of the rising tide of Estonian and Latvian
nationalism was clearly expressed in the following statement
of the German *Petersburger Zeitung* (May, 1905):

The Baltic Germans . . . will have to take the legal way of
appealing for help and support . . . They will appeal to the
[Russian] government, since they [the Baltic provinces] belong
to the Russian empire . . . The Russification policy in the . . .
Baltic provinces led to the arresting of its natural development
. . . which led to anarchy . . . The Baltic Germans do not need
artificial protection of their Germandom, but they ask the government not to destroy their Germandom artificially . . . We
do not expect to be defended against the numerically stronger
natives, but we will stay as long as we can in the position we
hope to defend . . . as long as there remains a spark of our old
Baltic spirit.[35]

Such a statement from the German press in Russia shows
how the German position changed to one of fearing the Estonians while appealing for the aid of their former enemy—
the Russian government. Nevertheless, the German Balts did
not lose their pride completely, since they still hoped to with-
stand the rising tide of nationalism, at least for a time. Some
hoped for a compromise with Tõnisson and the Estonian
middle class by offering to share the power. By dividing the
class interests of the Estonian people, the Balts hoped to up-
hold their privileges.

After the revolution Jaan Tõnisson became the popular
tribune of Estonian nationalism. He fought anything which
stood in the way of complete emancipation. Tõnisson particularly emphasized his idea of forming a united front

against German privilege. He fought Russification with
equal vehemence, though his language was modified because
of consorship. Together with Tõnisson, other men—church-
man Johan Kõpp, lawyer Kaarel Parts, theologian and educator Peeter Põld, journalist and critic Anton Jürgenstein,
poet Karl E. Sööt—were very active in fostering Estonian
social life after the 1905 revolution.[36] In his *Postimees* Tõnisson summarized how the Germans could show their good will
by helping the small Estonian people to build its national
culture. The Germans, he stated, should think of integrating
their cultural activities with those of the Estonian people,
and leave to the Estonians the management of political affairs.[37]

7. Aftermath of the 1905 Revolution

Despite the October Manifesto, the Russian government
did not free the press or fulfill its promises of local and national representation, from which the Estonian *bourgeoisie*
expected so much. Instead, the activities of the press and
various Estonian societies was rigidly controlled. The reaction following the revolution forced Estonian nationalism
underground. Even such innocent organizations as the *Karskuse Sõber* had great difficulty in continuing their activities.
The Russian government openly fought every political expression of Estonian nationalism, thus indirectly aiding the
German nobility.[38] The revolution in Estonia showed the
Russian government that it had greatly under estimated the
strength of Estonian nationalism when it aided Estonians
against the Baltic nobility throughout the previous century.
The revolution brought to light the dangerous leaning of the
Estonian people toward socialism and their burning desire
for political reforms, which seemed to the Tsar much more
dangerous than the Baltic German menace.[39] The Baltic
German press laid the guilt for the revolution upon the Estonian press, calling Jaan Tõnisson a nationalistic dema-
gogue, and accusing him of fostering hatred against the Ger-

man landowners.[40] Some German Balts believed that the
revolutionary ideas found entrance in Estonia through the
reforms of Alexander III, when many Russian governmental
officials and teachers came into the Baltic provinces, who
brought liberal and revolutionary ideas with them. An important factor in the 1905 revolutionary upheaval in the
Baltic provinces were, they believed, the ideas of "Land and
Freedom," spread by the Social-Revolutionaries, which
greatly undermined the possible German-Estonian cooperation.[41]

While the conservative and reactionary press in Germany
denounced the Estonian and Latvians for their uprising
against the German Balts, and collected money for the support of the Baltic nobles who lost their property, the only
German group who defended the Estonians and the Latvians
and condemned the brutal deeds of the Baltic nobles, was the
socialistic press.[42] Although Bebel and the *Vorwärts* represented only one, and not the largest, segment of the German
people, it nevertheless expressed the attitude of the democratic part of the German people and openly condemned the
German Baltic nobility for their part in the pacification of
the Baltic provinces by massacring the native Estonian and
Latvian population. Such an attitude, however, did not
change the attitude of the Baltic nobles towards the Estonians
and Latvians; nor did it, after 1905, influence Baltic German' policy of maintaining their dominant economic and
political position with the help of the Tsarist government,
by now frightened by the revolutionary spirit of the Estonians and Latvians. Crying over the loss of their castles and
their cattle, they again believed to be firmly entrenched,
thanks to the Russian military might, in their positions. That
their positions cracked as soon as the Romanov' empire collapsed was one of those miscalculations the Baltic nobility
made because they believed that history can be brought to a
standstill. That the 1905 revolution did not teach the nobles
anything, their frustrating attempts to hold the Baltic provinces at the end of the First World War showed clearly.

CHAPTER XI

The Road to Freedom

It was a long way from the aftermath of the Great Northern War to the 1905 Revolution. For the Estonian people the road was one of hardship, of struggle, but also of great successes. During those two centuries the little nation survived both Germanization and Russification, and the First World War found it ready to take over its own destiny—that of a free, independent Estonia. To understand the causes of such a development we have to consider the many phases of its development, each phase with its own problems and its own solutions.

If it should be asked how the Estonians could maintain their nationality against the pressures of Germanization during the eighteenth century, one can find the answer in their folk poetry. Through centuries the Estonian peasants adhered to their folk poetry. During the long winter months, when the whole family was sitting around the fire spinning, the women would sing ancient Estonian songs. This was the only diversion in their monotonous and miserable lives. Ancient folk poetry, full of descriptions of the free and heroic past, strengthened the spiritual life of the peasants.[1] While collecting folklore, the Estophils were strongly impressed by the militant spirit of those Estonian songs. As compared to the Latvians, the Estonians expressed much more adherence to their heroic past, their struggles and battles for independence.[2] Thus the Baltic Germans feared and respected the Estonians more than they did the Latvians, whom they considered more dependable but weaklings.

In the course of time, advancing Christianity had a negative effect on pagan folkways. As late as the first half of the eighteenth century, leaders of the Moravian Brethren fought the secret practice of pagan customs that still continued among Estonians.[3] During the years 1810-20 there developed among the wealthier Estonian peasants a secret society called *Püha Seltsirahvas* (Holy Brotherhood), which suppressed the singing of folk and worldly songs, thus hampering the preservation of folk poetry among the peasants.[4] Nevertheless, where the Brethren's religious leaders did not have complete control over the peasants, as well as among members of the Orthodox Church, the peasants were able to sing and thus preserve their folk poetry in complete freedom.[5] So one can see how the Estonians through their folklore managed to retain their national spirit. Their constant singing of Estonian songs and chanting of the national epic, the *Kalevipoeg,* kept alive their memory of past as a free people and preserved their hopes of again becoming free.[6]

A true renaissance of the Estonian culture could never have developed (as it did during the first half of the nineteenth century) without the help of the Estophils. Interest in Estonia and its culture received its first and strongest impetus from the publication of Johann Herder's *Stimmen der Völker,* a collection of the folk poetry of many peoples. Prior to Herder, even such an outstanding linguist as August Wilhelm Hupel did not show much interest in the preservation of Estonian folklore. Only after the work of the brothers Grimm, after Herder's search for folklore of all nations, and after the interest in folk poetry in Finland, did there develop a similar interest in Estonia on the part of several Estophils. The actual collecting of Estonian folk poetry began with the activities of the Estonian Learned Society.[7] Herder's importance in stimulating the work of the Society can never be minimized. His *Stimmen der Völker* aroused the interest of the Estophils in the naive and simple habits of peoples, and in preserving for mankind the cultural heritage of all nations, large and small. Thus Herder laid the foundation for the idea of the Estonian nationality—an idea later looked upon by German scholars with disdain.[8] From purely academic interest in the Estonian culture the Estophils, and later the Estonian Learned Society, entered the field of education. Estophils are remembered for their contribution to the spread of literacy.[9]

Folklore alone could not have enabled the Estonian people to survive the hardest of times and preserve their national character. In addition to folklore there followed the enlightened ideas of the Estophils, which, in turn, were influenced by the ideas behind the French Revolution. The impact of the French Revolution upon the Baltic provinces was great. The question of the dignity of man lost its academic character during the first decades of the nineteenth century. The issue of the rights of man to physical and spiritual equality was no longer a theoretical problem, but a very practical one, especially in light of the condition of the peasants. The issue of emancipation later became the source of difference between the liberal and the conservative Baltic Germans. The conservatives saw a danger of revolution in the slightest change in their existing privileges; only under the pressure of circumstances did they give in. The reforms of 1804-1819 were the first results of the impact of the French Revolution and the liberalism of the Estophils. Though they had little immediate and profound effect, they prepared the ground for the changes which took place during the second half of the century.

The first half of that century witnessed the sharp internal struggle among the Baltic Germans over the issue of maintaining their ancient privileges while at the same time promoting the emancipation of the Estonian people. Those decades saw the slow process of emancipation. Nominal freedom from serfdom cost the peasants additional economic hardship and insecurity—their case was similar to that of the emancipation of the Russian peasants after 1861. The continuing hardships of the 'forties and 'fifties resulted in mass conver-

sions to the Orthodox Church, emigration, and bloody revolts which, despite their ruinous economic effects, had some
positive force upon the development of the Estonian's state
of mind. His disappointment in the reforms, in the Russian
Orthodox Church, and in the Tsar increased the peasant's
determination to pave his own way to full economic emancipation by utilizing to a maximum the rights granted him by
the reforms.

During the second half of the nineteenth century, the peasant concentrated all his energy upon completing his economic
independence from his landlord. Working himself and his
family to the point of death, the peasant tried hard to pay
off his debt to the landlord. His goal was a distant one, and
sometimes he never lived to see it attained. But the theoretical possibility of becoming free, as remote as it was, became
one of the strongest factors in promoting the peasant's economic emancipation, which in its turn pointed the way towards the cultural renaissance of the people.

The basis laid by the Estophils for the national awakening
helped to bring forth from among the peasants a nucleus of
Estonian intelligentsia. The second half of the nineteenth
century saw the crystallization of a national ideology. First
expressed by the pioneer of Estonian nationalism, Voldemar
Jannsen, it was later strengthened through the political leadership of Carl Robert Jakobson. During the 'sixties and
'seventies, the idea acquired a more definite shape through
the political struggle between the moderate Jannsen and the
radical Jakobson, and gained more ground among the people.
At first the Russification gave Estonians false hopes of aid in
their national cause against the Baltic nobility and German
middle class. Jakobson did not live long enough to witness
the disappointment of those hopes. But the following generation of Villem Reiman, Jakob Hurt, and Michkel Weske
accepted the challenge of Russification and used every available means in promoting cultural and economic emancipation.

One can trace the changing reactions of the Baltic Germans through the latter part of the century as the liberals and conservatives tried in vain to find a solution to the Baltic question. For the conservatives, as seen by Schirren and his followers, the Baltic province had to remain what they had been for seven centuries: the eastern citadel of Germandom. The majority of the Baltic Germans supported Schirren in his struggle against the onslaught of the Pan-Slavists and their extreme exponents Iurii Samarin and Mikhail Katkov.

There were a few liberal Balts who openly supported the cause of Estonian nationalism and culture. Such a man was Georg Julius Schultz. He often encouraged Friedrich Kreutzwalk to continue with the collection of parts of the *Kalevipoeg*. Among the German Balts Schultz was an exception, a man who loved the Estonian peasant and who fully supported his cultural and economic emancipation.[10]

The growing national spirit was received by the Baltic Germans with great surprise and disappointment. Many tried to find the cause for such a development, especially those liberals who believed that the Estonian people, or at least its intelligentsia, were destined for Germanization. They accused the conservative nobles of having stopped the trend toward Germanization by a superior attitude. The conservatives based this attitude on their fear that the Estonians would become too proud if they learned the German language and adopted the German culture. The liberals insisted that the times offered a wonderful chance to promote Germanization. The very fact that the Estonians belonged to the Lutheran Church should have promoted such a trend. But the negative attitude of the Conservatives and the lack of German peasants in the Baltic provinces destroyed such an opportunity. By the beginning of the twentieth century, when Russia had begun to intervene actively in Baltic policies, it was too late, since Estonian national consciousness had become a formidable factor.[11] The cries of the Baltic nobles grew louder with their increasing strug-

gle against the Russian Government during the last quarter
of the nineteenth century. Faced by the opposition of both
the Estonian people and the Russian government, the Baltic
nobles lost more and more the supremacy over the Baltic
provinces. The liberals continued to insist upon the great
cultural mission of the Germans in the Baltic provinces,
which, they argued, would not belong to Western civilization
without the pioneering work of the Germans.[12] Conservatives and liberals alike staunchly defended the progressive
mission of the Baltic nobility in promoting economic emancipation of the Estonians (and Latvians).[13] By the end of
the nineteenth century the German Balts claimed to have
contributed to the private character of the Estonian peasant
village and the progressive system of monetary rent by their
good will.[14] Why then, they often asked themselves, is the
Estonian peasant so ungrateful, and full of hate? Some believed, that the answer lay in the historic difference between
the well-to-do noble and the struggling Estonian peasant.
While the well-to-do peasant expressed his dissatisfaction
the poor peasant remained quiet.[15] The Germans attributed
growing nationalism to the hurt feeling of the Estonian that,
despite his abilities and his improved standard of life, he
was not permitted by the German minority to participate in
local government. Here some Germans saw the nobles'
guilt.[16]

At the turn of the century, the consolidation of the Estonian national forces, the economic growth of the peasantry,
and the emergence of a new Estonian middle class were
slowly but steadily pushing the German middle class from
its ancient position. The Baltic Germans met this menace
as well as they could. The nobility fought for its privileges
not only against the Estonians, but also against its own
middle class. The cause was lost, for the towns already had
an Estonian majority. The Estonian middle class was economically sound, and educationally on a par with the German middle class or the middle classes of neighboring coun-

tries. Only in the number of professional people—doctors, engineers, agronomists, and technicians—did the Estonians lag behind the Germans. This was due to the youth of the Estonian intelligentsia and the lack of facilities for professional training. Estonian workers and servants made up the strongest element in the cities.[17]

For the Estonian intellectual the struggle for existence against a well-established German intelligentsia was a bitter one. A great number migrated into Russia, where they could secure a better economic life than in their homeland.[18] Those remaining never lost contact with their own middle class; they looked to them for aid against the German intelligentsia. At the same time the rising Estonian middle class realized the value of an ally against their German competitors and fully supported the new intelligentsia. Thus it was natural that the Estonian intelligentsia assume leadership of the political movement.[19]

By 1905 the majority of the peasants were heavily burdened because of their debts assumed by becoming independent landowners, also because of the steady division of land within constantly growing families. The cultural needs of the peasants grew steadily after their emancipation; they created their own cultural and professional institutions despite economic and political hardship.[20] The worst off were the landless peasants—about 10 per cent of the rural population. Having no steady employment, they wandered from village to city in search of work. Always before them was the impossible dream of acquiring land of their own. The fact that they would perform any labor for very little pay kept wages low.[21]

Overpopulation in rural areas during the latter part of the nineteenth century resulted in a steady flow of peasants into the cities, swelling the ranks of the industries and crafts. The result was the emergence of a larger Estonian working class by the beginning of the twentieth century. The workers were following the organizational developments of labor in other countries. Under the pressure of the Russian reaction prior to the 1905 revolution such development became exceedingly difficult: the labor press was steadily suppressed, the newspapers closed, and the editors arrested and sent to Siberia. The economic lot of the workers was poor. There were no laws defending them against exploitation at the hands of German and Estonian employers.

The struggle of all classes was directed primarily against the Baltic Germans. Suppressed for centuries, the peasants had nothing but hatred for the nobility. At the same time the Estonian city-dwellers recognized in the German middle class their common enemy. The rising Estonian merchants and craftsmen waged bitter competitive war against their German counterparts. The Estonian intelligentsia fought a well-entrenched and resentful German rival. Since the factory owners were for the most part Germans, as were the foremen and technical personnel, the Estonian workers found themselves pitted against Germans.[22] Having family ties in the villages and on the farms, the workers sympathized with the peasants and shared their hatred for the German Balts.[23] The class struggle became interwoven with national hatred.

The 1905 outburst of hatred on the part of the workers and landless peasants shocked and frightened the Baltic Germans. The first fearful reaction was the expression of vague, repentant ideas about "giving more equality to the Estonians," which disappeared during the suppression of the revolution and the following period of reaction. Afterwards, some Germans began to search their past relations with the Estonians, trying to find justification for the preservation of their political monopoly in the Baltic provinces. They contended that they had always desired reforms for the peasant, but that the Tsarist government had opposed their good intentions. This was not true of the nobility as a class; only a few far-sighted liberals helped to achieve reform. That the German contention was false can be proved by the records of the *Landtage* (Baltic German provincial councils). Neither the nobility nor the Russian government promoted far-reaching reforms in the Baltic provinces, nor did the Russian administration help to realize them. The revolution itself is the best witness against the contention of the German nobles.[24]

Some German Balts openly admitted their guilt, however. One wrote in an anonymous pamphlet, *Das baltische und die Vorschlage zur seiner Lösung,* that the German Balts should have realized their common interests with the Estonians, and thus avoided the violence of the year 1905. But at the same time this so-called liberal author added that such understanding might have saved the specific character of the Baltic provinces.[25] He added that the industrialization of the Baltic provinces had increased national and social differences. He accused the Estonian and Latvian revolutionary parties of straining relations by their propaganda.[26] Thus we can see how little the Baltic Germans understood the causes of the 1905 revolution.

While the Baltic Germans were counting their economic losses caused by the revolution, the conservative German press in Germany continued to call for the preservation of their brethren in the Baltic provinces. Political literature was full of the feudal spirit of the Baltic nobles, drawing a picture of the Baltic provinces as populated by a strong German majority. The conservative German newspapers painted the Estonians as a small minority jeopardizing German life and limb with the help of the evil Tsar. One need only glance at the statistical facts to observe the inaccuracy of the German conservative press in Germany. In 1910 the population of Estonia consisted of 1,195,000 Estonians and 25,000 Germans. The Germans made up only 1.5 per cent of the population. Of them only 4700 (0.23 per cent) were nobles and an additional 300 were clergymen, of whom half lived in the towns. The remainder, 20,000 Germans, belonged to the middle class and the intelligentsia.[27] Such were the facts, as opposed to what the conservative press in Germany tried to impress upon the world and the German people. In Germany only the liberal and democratic press denounced the Baltic Germans and expressed sympathy with the Estonians and Latvians.[28]

For the sake of truth the impression should not be left that the entire Estonian population was against the Germans. Some tried to adopt the German culture and way of life. We have already mentioned the Estonian well-to-do among the peasant and middle classes. But there were also *Kadakasaksad* among the students. In one of its publications the *Teataja* sharply criticized the behavior of some members of the student corporations. The *Teataja* stated that the Estonian and Latvian student corporations were imitating the German. The newspaper added that the Estonian intellectual in his later life likewise imitated the German in his behavior towards the Estonian people.[29]

Despite the differences among political factions within the Estonian people, the 1905 Revolution brought to light an expression of the national consciousness which they held in common: a desire for self-determination, for freedom from both German and Russian overlordship. The following reactionary period revealed elements of opportunism; such cases were survivors of the slave mentality of the not-too-distant Estonian past. The revolution washed away with blood and tears many remnants of the slave psychology, preparing the Estonian people for its final effort toward complete emancipation from both the Baltic Germans and Tsarist Russia.

CONCLUSION

The Estonian People—From the Aftermath of the 1905 Revolution Until the First Soviet Occupation of 1940

The suppression of Estonian national aspirations after 1905 did not eliminate the desire to become free from both German and Russian domination. Although politically suppressed by the Tsar's police, the Estonians maintained and carried on their activities in the field of economics, social work, and the expansion of their national culture.

Cooperative banks to help small businessmen, agricultural banks, milk, and other cooperatives were organized and expanded. A 1906 law permitted the establishment of Estonian private secondary schools, several higher elementary schools, and the first Girls' Gymnasium. In the field of literature two groups carried on a lively and friendly competition: men of letters of the old generation, centering around the newly established literary monthly *Estonian Literature (Eesti Kirjandus)*, and a more rebellious group of young Estonian poets and writers who called themselves "Young Estonia" *(Noor Eesti)*. A museum called "The Estonian Peoples' Museum" *(Eesti Rahva Muuseum)*, which became the national shrine of the Estonian people, was established near Tartu. Here artifacts, tools, national clothes, and national folk art from the earliest times were assembled and exhibited. Estonian theaters sprung up all over the country: in Tartu, Tallinn, Pärnu, and many smaller towns.

The outbreak of World War I kindled the Estonians' hopes, and when the February Revolution of 1917 overthrew the Tsar, they did not fail to take advantage of the situation.

Under a Bill of the Provisional Russian Government of Kerensky, which permitted national minorities to establish their own administrative agencies, the Estonian and Livonian provinces were for the first time in the history of the Estonian people united under one administration headed by Jaan Poska, then mayor of Tallinn. On July 1, 1917 a demo-cratically elected Estonian Diet met in Tallinn. It elected its own government with Konstantin Päts as its head.

After the October Revolution the Estonian government declared on November 28, 1917, its withdrawal from the Russian State. On February 24, 1918, the Estonian Council of Elders declared Estonia an independent democratic state.

The Treaty of Brest-Litovsk signed by Russian and Imperial Germany on March 3, 1918, turned over the Baltic countries (Latvia and Estonia) to Germany. Although Estonian independence was recognized by England and France (May, 1919) and Italy (June, 1918), the German occupational forces ignored the declaration of independence of the Estonian government, forced the Estonian governmental agencies underground and into exile, and arrested several national leaders—among them Konstantin Päts—who did not manage to escape or hide.

Imperial Germany's defeat and surrender in November, 1918, made it again possible for the Estonian government to take over the country. Released from a German concentration camp, Konstantin Päts again organized a cabinet. Despite the collapse of Imperial Germany, the German forces in Estonia, supplemented by local German Balts, attempted to maintain their grip on the country. Headed by General von der Goltz, the newly established *Landeswehr* fought the newly established Estonian and Latvian armies. While fighting the *Landeswehr* the young Estonian Republic faced another formidable enemy, the Red Army, which crossed into

Estonia on November 1, 1918. For a time more than half of the territory of the Estonian Republic was occupied by the Red Army. With the help and support of Finnish, Danish and Swedish volunteers as well as naval and armament support from England, and under the able leadership of general Johan Laidoner, the Estonian army, consisting essentially of tens of thousands of volunteers, succeeded in routing both the Red Army and the Landeswehr from Estonia. In the peace treaty of Tartu, signed on February 2, 1920, Soviet Russia recognized Estonian sovereignty and renounced all claims to Estonian territory.

The War of Liberation—as the war against the *Landeswehr* and the Red Army was later called—drained Estonia both economically and of human resources. But Estonia achieved its independence—a dream cherished for centuries—and the Estonian people immediately moved toward restoring and rebuilding their economic, administrative and cultural life.

Soon afterwards Estonia was recognized by the Allies *de Jure;* on January 26, 1921 by England, France and Italy; on July 28, 1922 by the United States. On November 22, 1921 Estonia was admitted to the League of Nations.

Prior to its *de Jure* recognition and entrance into the League of Nations, the Estonian Republic moved toward establishing its political foundation, the first Estonian Constitution. New elections were held to the Constituent Assembly in 1919 and work was begun on the writing of the Constitution.

Adopted in 1920, it provided for one Legislative Assembly *(Riigikogu)*, a referendum, and an executive to be composed from various political parties. No provision was made for a President or Head of State. Instead, the Prime Minister was to head the government. The executive was especially weak by making it dependent upon a vote of confidence by the Legislative Assembly. In addition to the writing and adopting of the constitution, a series of other important laws were passed. Among the most important was an Agrarian Law which provided for the distribution of land. The large estates of the German Baltic nobility were distributed among the Estonian landless peasants, for which, however, the former owners were compensated.

The Estonian Republic faced its first internal crisis, in 1924. On December 1, 1924, several hundred Estonian Communists, most of whom were smuggled by the Soviets across the border, attempted a military overthrow of the Estonian government in Tallinn. The coup was crushed by the Estonian army and military cadets in a few hours, but is resulted in the outlawing of the Estonian Communist Party and the growth of the political trend toward the right and away from political democracy.

Between 1919 and 1933 Estonian political life was in a constant state of change due to the lack of an effective executive as well as the political immaturity of the country. During this period twenty-one governments rose and fell, many of them short-lived. Such political instability greatly handicapped the economic growth of the young Republic, which was thus ill-prepared for the coming of the Great Depression of the Thirties.

The failure of democracy in Europe and the rise of Fascism and Nazism, coupled with growing unemployment in Estonia, did not fail to affect Estonia's political life.

As a result of the failure of the First Constitution to stabilize political life, Estonia entered a period of political and economic crisis which led to substantial changes in its governmental system. Widespread unemployment, the lowering of wages among governmental workers, and the frequent changes of governments created a desire among many Estonians to strengthen the power of the executive. In August 1932, a referendum was held to alter the Constitution by establishing the position of a president who would, as many people hoped, "become master in the house". It failed to get the necessary votes and another attempt was made in June 1933 which also failed. During this year, the Estonian government of Jaan Tõnisson was especially attacked by a newly organized group, the s.c. *VABS'*—The War of Liberation Solders' League. Originally organized to protect the economic interest of the ex-servicemen, the *VABS'* soon became the rally force of all right-wing groups in Estonia. Strongly influenced by Fascisf and Nazism, using the demagoguery of the latter, the *VABS'* in their 1931 congress decided to change the Constitution and establish a Head of State with authoritarian powers. Artur Sirk, a lawyer, became their head. Admitting into their organization not only ex-servicemen but everyone who would subscribe to their ideology, the *VABS'* by 1933 became one of the strongest political groups. After the failure of the second attempt to revise the Constitution, the *VABS'* proposed their own version. After a well-prepared political campaign, the *VABS'* revision of the Constitution was adopted by a large majortiy held in a referendum in October, 1933. Since this referendum turned out to be a vote of non-confidence to the government of Jaan Tõnisson, the latter resigned and Konstantin Päts took the office of Prime Minister.

Confident of their power and sure of mass support, the *VABS'* openly agitated to substitute the government of Päts with a purely *VABS'* one. Konstantin Päts, a moderate democrat, feared that the country would fall into the hands of a totalitarian group and eventually turn Estonia into a puppet of Nazi-Germany. Wishing to prevent such a change, Päts used the powers the new Constitution gave him. On March 12, 1934, he proclaimed a state of emergency. The *VABS'* leadership then proceeded with the preparation of coup d'état. Päts let the *VABS'* get ready for the military takeover while keeping a careful watch on them with the help of the secret police and the assured support of the Commander in Chief of the Estonian army, General Johan Laidoner. When the leaders of the coup assembled in their secret headquarters in Tallin on December 8, 1935, Päts apprehended them a few hours before they were going to take over the government.

Although the leader of the *VABS'*, Artur Sirk, and several others of the movement succeeded in escaping abroad, the government of Päts subsequently rounded up several hundred of the *VABS'* elite. Soon afterwards the government put them on public trial, where the ideological and financial ties between the VABS' and the National Socialist German Workers Party were revealed. During the trial, the leadership of the *VABS'* denounced each other and especially their leader Sirk, who while escaping, managed to depart with the entire treasury of the VABS' organization.

After having publicly discredited the *VABS'* in the eyes of the Estonian people, the government of Päts treated the *VABS'* leniently. With the exception of a few, the majority of the arrested received short prison terms. Their leader, Artur Sirk, soon afterwards committed suicide in exile in Switzerland. Although the danger of Fascism was eliminated, the political situation in Estonia remained unstable. Using his dictatorial powers Konstantin Päts dissolved the National Assembly and all political parties and ran the country by decrees, preparing the ground work for a new Constitution. In order to gain popular support for his regime and for a new Constitution, Päts founded a new organization, the *Patriotic League (Isamma Liit).* This organization embraced the old Conservative Peasant Party and most middle-of-the-road parties, with the middle classes, business and profsesional people, following and supporting the former. Using various patriotic organizations—such as the *Defense Union (Kait-seliit)*—a paramilitary organization established after the Communist coup of December 1, 1924; the *Young Eagles (Noored Kotkad)*—a patriotic youth group similar to that of the Scouts; and various farmer organizations—the *Patriotic League* appealed for national unity and for economic and political cooperation among the various social and economic groups in order to stabilize the young Republic's economic and political life. While the *Patriotic League* carried on its organizational activities unhampered by political rivals, Konstantin

Päts moved the country toward a semi-corporate state. Workers and professional groups were ordered to form corporate bodies all totalling 18 different corporate chambers. When the National Assembly drafted a new Constitution in 1937, it was easily approved in a referendum and put into force on January 1, 1938.

The new Constitution consisted of two chambers: a House of Representatvies (*Riigivolikogu*) with 80 members, and a State Council (*Riiginoukogu*) consisting of 40 members of whom ten were to be appointed by the President.

Each chamber was elected for five years. The Constitution provided for a president to be elected for five years. On April 23, 1938, Konstantin Päts was elected the first President under the new Constitution.

Between 1938 and 1940 Estonia remained a one-party state, with the President having almost dictatorial powers. Under Päts it was run in a paternalistic way, with limited freedom of speech, limited activities for unions, and with a mildly censored press. In comparison with Lithuania and Latvia, where the regimes of Smetona and Ulmanis did not permit any criticism of the government, President Päts' regime was benevolently authoritarian. Many Estonians criticized the President for having destroyed democracy, but at the same time they had to concede that Konstantin Päts did save Estonia from an outright fascist-nazi takeover by the *VABS*.

Economically the new government gave its full support to the farmers—about 60% of the population—while letting the workers remain on the bottom of the economic totempole. Various economic measures promoted the welfare of the Estonian farmer during the regime of Päts: the establishment of numerous peasant credit banks, which provided thousands of farmers with long and short-term loans; lowering the taxes for newly established farms; helping the farmers to sell their agricultural goods abroad through various barter agreements, and maintaining high price support abroad.

The greatest success the young Estonian Republic achieved

was in developing a truly Estonian culture including an educational system, arts, and sciences. For the promotion of cultural life the government established an *Estonian Culture Fund (Eesti Kultuurikapital)*. It drew its income from various taxes on commodities such as liquor and tobacco. The Fund helped to promote the growth of an Estonian national theater, fine arts, journalism, literature, and sports. To eliminate the worries of livelihood from outstanding Estonian artists, musicians and writers, a governmental Pension Fund was established in 1935. During the twenty years of Estonian independence a first-class educational system was established and enlarged. This system included primary schools (obligatory until 14 years), various gymnasiums (secondary schools), technical (profession) schools, music academies and art schools, and the two higher institutions of learning, Tartu University and Tallinn University (Technical). The pride of Estonian nationhood was its treatment of national minorities. Although predominantly Estonian (about 87%) it had about 100,000 Russians, 15,000 Germans, 5000 Jews, and about 1000 Swedes. Strictly adhereing to the Wilsonian principles of respecting the rights of national minorities (which were incorporated into the charter of the League of Nations), the Estonian Laws of Cultural Autonomy, passed in 1925 and 1931, gave the national minorities full cultural and religious autonomy.

Each national minority developed its own national schools and religious institutions, supported by the Estonian government and by taxes from their own respective group.

Unlike other newly established European countries like Poland or Hungary, relations between the Estonian government and the national minorities remained cordial and friendly. And although there existed some dissatisfaction among the Russians, Germans, and Jews because of lack of economic opportunities, it was not the result of an outright anti-minority policy by the Estonian government, but rather the lack of economic opportunities in general for the fast growing Estonian middle classes and professionals.

In its relations with Soviet Russia the Estonian Republic was cool but cordial. As a result of the Molotov-Ribbentrop Pact of August 23, 1939, Estonia was compelled by the Soviet Union to sign the Soviet-Estonian Mutual Assistance Pact. This Pact enabled the Soviets to establish military and naval bases in Estonia. Thus the first step toward the occupation of Estonia was made by the Soviet Union. Although the former refrained from doing anything to provoke the Soviet Union, it received, on June 16, 1940, an ultimatum in which Estonia was accused of violating the Mutual Assistance Pact because it has joined a military alliance with Latvia and Lithuania. The Soviet Union demanded from Estonia, among other things, the establishment of a new Estonian government friendlier to the Soviet Union, and the right of free passage of Soviet troops through Estonia. However, without having waited for a reply, the Soviet Government ordered its troops into Estonia. The Red Army crossed the borders on June 17 and completed the occupation by June 22.

The general mood of the Estonian people was shock, surprise, and anger. If President Päts would have ordered the Estonian army to resist and called the people to fight for their independence, he would have found mass support among the population. Realizing the hopelessness of the situation, President Päts appealed over the radio to the Estonian people to maintain calm and face fate as they had faced it many times before. Within a month, on July 22, 1940, Estonia was proclaimed a Soviet Republic by the newly formed Estonian Communist government. Thus ended the existence of the young Estonian independent republic. During the twenty years of its brief life, despite economic and political instability and lack of administrative experience, the Estonian people proved to the world and to themselves that a small nation of one million not only had the right to self-determination, but also could maintain its political and economic independence, develop its own national culture, and become a respected member of the family of nations.

Although the tide of history did engulf the Estonian people as had happened so often before and the political and cultural life of Estonia as an independent nation was extinguished by its powerful neighbor, the spark of hope, as cherished by Estonians for centuries under German and Tsarist domination, still remains in the hearts of each Estonian.

NOTES

Preface

* The "Juniper Germans" were nicknamed contemptuously for the abundant evergreen which never attains a great height. Having renounced their nationality and adopted German ways, they were denounced as traitors and held in contempt, especially by the younger generation of Estonians.

Chapter I

1. J. G. Willigerod, *Geschichte Ehstlands'*, Reval, 1830, 278-279; Leonid A. Arbusow, *Ocherk istorii Lifliandii, Estliandii i Kurliandii (Outline History of Livonia, Estonia, and Courland)*, St. Petersburg, 1912, p. 229. On the economic and religious conditions in the Estonian villages the author wrote: "After 1710 military operations ceased in Livonia and Estonia, but the upkeep of many garrisons, stationed in both provinces, ruined the population . . . For several decades after the end of the Great Northern War the Estonian peasants did not have ministers in the villages. Very often one pastor had to take care of more than five communities. Often those pastors did not have any religious education, but achieved positions through graft and protectionism."

2. Zieldonis Ligers, *Geschichte der baltischen Stadte*, Bern, 1948, 6. "As a result of the Northern War the Black Death took the lives of most of the 15,000 citizens of Reval . . . In the year 1708 the Czar ordered the transfer of its citizens [*i.e.* the citizens of Dorpat] into Russia, and the destruction of the fortifications in Dorpat, since he suspected that the Swedes might recapture the city. The transportation of Dor-

pat's citizenry took place on the 18th of February. After several days the city was burned down. Only in 1714 was it permitted to the citizens of Dorpat to return to the ruins of their city."

3. Otto Fabian Wrangell's *Chronik von Ehstland,* Dorpat, 1845, 199-213; Reinhart Wittram, *Baltische Geschichte,* München, 1954, 133-136.

4. H. Diedrich, "Garlieb Merkel als Bekämpfer der Leibeigenschaft und seine Vorgänger" in *Baltische Monatsschrift,* vol. 19 (1870), 40.

5. E. F. Dubiuk, "Krestianskoie dvizenie v Lifliandii vo vtoroi Polovine XVIII Veka" (Peasant movements in Livonia during the second half of the XVIII century), *Istoricheskiie Zapiski,* (Historical notes) Vol. 13 (1942), 175-207.

6. John Hampden Jackson, *Estonia,* London, 1948, 71-72.

7. Johann Georg Eisen, "Eines livländischen Patrioten Beschreibung der Leibeigenschaft wie solche in Livland uber die Bauern eingefuhrt ist," in Müller's, *Sammlung der russischen Geschichte,* 1776. In this book Eisen criticized the system of manorial labor, which, he believed, corrupted the peasants, destroyed their dignity, and made the peasant an animal. Eisen published (about 1750) a book in the Estonian language, the so-called *Karneri Ramat* (Garden Book), in which he gave the peasants many practical directions for planting and taking care of a garden, with special reference to each particular fruit and its care. The further development of gardening among the Estonian peasants was largely a result of Eisen's helpful suggestions.

8. *Eesti Biograafiline Leksikon* (Estonian Biographical Dictionary), Tartu, 1926-1929, 147-148.

9. Leonid Arbusow, *op. cit.,* 254-255.

10. Ojamaa and Varmas, *Eesti Ajalugu* (History of Estonia), Stockholm, 1946, 185.

11. *Ibid.,* 186-189; Herbord Karl Friedrich von Bienenstamm, *Geographischer Abriss der drei deutschen Ostseeprovinzen Russlands,* Riga, 1826, 38-43.

12. *Ibid.,* 40.

13. Julius Eckard, *Livland im achtzehnten Jahrhundert,* Leipzig, 1876, 320-321.

14. Westren-Doll, "Abgötterei zu Ausgang der Schwedischen und Beginn der Russischen Zeit." in *Sitzungsberichte der Gelehrten Ehstnischen Gesellschaft,* Dorpat, 1925, 7-25. "During the first half of the eighteenth century many Estonians prac-

ticed paganism, which could be seen from the sacrifice places at the Catholic churches and which was still continued by the Estonian population while (being) protestants."

15. Julius Eckard, *op. cit.*, 165.
16. Friedrich Wiegand, *Siebenhundert Jahre baltischer Kirchengeschichte*, Gütersesh, 1921, 38-39.
17. Julius Eckard, *op. cit.*, 164-166.
18. *Ibid.*, 216-246.
19. G. Suits, *Eesti Kirjanduslugu* (History of Estonian Literature), Lund, 1953, 51-56.
20. *Ibid.*, 45-46.

Chapter II

1. Leonid Arbusow, *Ocherk istorii Lifliandii, Estliandii i Kurliandii,* St. Petersburg 1912, 225-232; 234; Julius Eckardt, *Livland im achtzehnten Jahrhundert,* Leipzig. 1876, 415-428.
2. See Chapter I, page 27-30; Ojamaa and Varmas, *Eesti Ajalugu* (History of Estonia) Stockholm, 1946, 191-194. Julius Eckardt, *Livland im achtzehnten Jahrhundert,* 232-247.
3. Gustav Suits, *Eesti Kirjanduslugu* (History of Estonian Literature), Lund, 1953, 76-123.
4. Ojamaa and Varmas, *op. cit.*, 182-184.
5. (Anon.,) "Das Volksschulwesen in Liv-Est- und Kurland," in *Baltische Monatsschrift,* vol. 21, (1872) 534.
6. *Ibid.*, p. 534.
7. J. Hampden Jackson, *Estonia,* London, 1941, p. 27. Ojamaa and Varmas, *Eesti Ajalugu,* Reinhard Wittram, *Baltische Geschichte,* München, 1953, 167.
8. *Ibid.*, pp. 158-161. Hans Kruus, *Grundriss der Geschichte des Estnischen Volkes,* Tartu, 1932, 53-69.
9. Hans Kruus, *op. cit.*, 62-68, 70-71. Reinhard Wittram, *op. cit.*, 160-162.
10. Hans Kruus, *op. cit.*, 79; Ojamaa and Varmas, *op. cit.*, 217.
11. Reinhard Wittram, *op. cit.*, 160-161.
12. J. G. Kohl, *Die deutsch-russischen Ostseeprovinzen oder Natur-und Völkerleben in Kur-, Esthland, und Livland.* Dresden und Leipzig, 1841, Vol. I, II.
13. *Ibid.*, 193.
14. *Ibid.*, 202.
15. *Ibid.*, 205.

16. *Ibid.*, 207.
17. *Ibid.*, p. 226.
18. *Ibid.*, 226; Hans Kruus, *op. cit.*, 48.
19. Heinrich Rosenthal, *Kulturbestrebungen des estnischen Volkes während eines Menschenalters,* Reval, 1912, 10.
20. *Ibid.*, 10.
 * See preface.
21. *Ibid.*, 10.
22. *Ibid.*, 10.
23. Jackson, *Estonia,* London, 1941, 92.
24. *Ibid.*, 92-93.
25. Herbord Karl Friedrich von Bienenstamm, *Geographische Abriss der drei deutschen Ostsee-Provinzen Russlands,* Riga, 1826, 41.
26. Ojamaa and Varmas, *Eesti Ajalugu,* Stockholm, 1946, 203-204.
27. *Ibid.*, 199-200.
28. Hans Kruus, *op. cit.*, 48-49.
29. Ojamaa and Varmas, *op. cit.*, 203.
30. [von Neander] *Die Deutsche Universität Dorpat im Lichte der Geschichte und der gegenwart,* Leipzig, 1882, 55-58.
31. H. Rosenthal, *op. cit.*, 14-15.
32. J. G. Kohl, *op. cit.*, 306.
33. Reinhard Wittram, *op. cit.*, 192-198.
34. "Die Nationalitätenfrage" in *Baltische Monatsschrift,* vol. 13, (1864), 568-575.
35. Kohl, *op. cit.*, 312.
36. *Ibid.*, 313.
37. *Ibid.*, 333.
38. *Ibid.*, 334.
39. V. von Reutz, "Der Ehste und sein Herr," in *Baltische Monatsschrift,* vol. 5 (1862), 128.

Chapter III

1. Ojamaa and Varmas, *Eesti ajalugu,* Stockholm, 1946, 198.
2. Jüri Ulnots, *Grundzüge der Agrargeschichte Estlands,* Tartu, 1935, 142.
3. x., [Alexander Buchholtz], *Fünfzig Jahre Russischer Verwaltung in den Baltischen Provinzen,* Leipzig, 1833, 44-45. Paul Hunfalvy, *Reise in den Ostsee provinzen Russlands,* Leipzig, 1874, 105-106.

4. x., [Alexander Buchholtz] *Funfzig Jahre Russischer Verwaltung in den Baltischen Provinzen*, 81-112.

5. Reinhard Wittram, *Baltische Geschichte*, München, 1954, 185-186. Also: P. Hunfalvy, *op. cit.*, 109.

6. J. Uluots, *op. cit.*, 151-152.

7. *Eesti Biograafiline Leksikon*, Tartu, 1929, 98-99; 449; Reinhard Wittram, *Meinungskämpfe im baltischen Deutschtum während der Reformepoche des 19. Jahrhunderts, Riga*, 1934, 8-14.

8. Julius Eckardt, *Die baltischen Provinzen Russlands*, Leipzig, 1869, 424-5.

9. W. von Bock, "Reinhold Johann Ludwig Samson von Himmelstiern," in *Baltische Monatsschrift*, vol. 2, (May 1860) 1-39. Samson's main concern was the emancipation of the peasants. Since his beginning career as a public servant in 1802, he participated in working out the project of the liberation of the peasants. He was the first one to propose the complete emancipation of the peasants of Livonia during the session of the *Landtag,* on June 1, 1818, which the latter accepted unanimously on the 27th of June, 1818. Samson's sympathies with the peasants cooled off during the 40's and, though he still supported the emancipation of the Livonian peasants, it was more a matter "of reason than of feelings," as he himself expressed in his diary.

10. J. Uluots, *op. cit.*, 149-150.

11. *Ibid.*, 154-156

12. Jackson, *Estonia*, 98-99.

13. Heinrich Resenthal, *Kulturbestrebungen des estnischen Volkes*, Reval, 1912, 27-28: Durch diese Acte (that is the reforms of 1816-1819) wurde den Bauern die persönhnliche Freiheit und Freizügrigkeit gewährt, im allgemeinen aber besserte sich ihre Lage nicht wesentlich. Sie mussten als entgelt für die Scholle, die sie ernähren sollte, ihrem bisherigen Herrn auch ferner noch Frondienste leisten. Freilich Geld und Gut besassen sie nicht, und das Land sollte ihnen nich geschenkt werden. Ihr einziges Besitztum bestand in ihrer Arbeitskraft, und diese wurde an Stelle einer Pachtzahlung in Berechnung gezogen. Die Arbeitsleistungen wurden genau normiert und dadurch vieler Wilkür vorgebeugt, aber die Anforderungen waren immens hoch bemessen. Nach der estlandischen Bauernverordnung vom Jahre 1857 Articel 127 hatte der Pachter eines mittelgrossen Bauerhofes an Frone zu leisten: im Laufe des Jahres 250 Fustage, das Aus-

dreschen des Heskorns, kleine Naturalabgaben und die Spinnerei, und 250 Anspannstage (Arbeit mit einem dem Bauer gehörigen Pferde). Die 'kleinen' Naturalabgaben betrugen: 1 Pud Flachs, 1 Pud Hanf, 1 Pud Garn, ein Sack, in welchem 1 1/5 Tschwert Roggen raumt, ein Fuder Heu von 15 Pud, 1 Pud Stroh, ein altes Schaf, ein junges Schaf, eine Gans ein Huhn, 100 Eier, und 1 Pfund Butter oder Talg. Die Spinnerei bestand aus: entweder 1) drei Pfund Flachs zu feinem Garn, oder 2) sechs Pfund Flachs zu mittelfeinem Garm, oder 3) 12 Pfund Flachs zu grobem Garn zu verspinnen, 4) 20 Pfund Hede zu verspinnen, und darans 30 Arschin Leinwand von 18 Werschok Breite zu weben, oder endlich 5) 20 Pfund Wolle zu verspinnen und daraus 22½ Arschin Bauertuch 18 Werschk breit zu weben. Da das jahr nicht 500 sondern hochstens 300 Arbeitstage enthält, so ist es klar, dass eine einzelne Person diese Forderungen nicht erfüllen konnte. Der Bauernwirt musste daher die Arbeitskräfte seiner Familie ausnutzen und ein mehr oder weniger zahlreiches Gesinde erhalten und beköstigen, um die erforderliche Fronarbeit zu bewältigen. Ausserdem musste er aber auch Zeit und Kräfte erübrigen für die Bearbeitung der in Pacht genommenen Felder, aus deren Ertragen der Unterhalt für die Familie und das gesamte Gesinde gewonnen wurde. Die Last der Frone war also nicht minder drückend als die Leieeigenschaft ....."

14. Helmut Speer, *Das Bauernschulwesen im Governement Estland,* Tartu, 1936, 97-98.
15. *Eesti Biograafiline Leksikon,* Tartu, 1929, 605.
16. H. Rosenthal, *op. cit.,* 36.
17. *Eesti Biograafiline Leksikon,* 1929, 140-141.
18. *Ibid.,* 32.
19. *Ibid.,* 33-34.
20. *Ibid.,* 34.
21. Heinrich Krummer, "Der Proletarier-Character der Bäuerlichen Ackerbau-Industrie in Livland und Estland," in *Baltische Monatsschrift,* vol. II (1860), 104.
22. Bernard Uxüll zu Fickel, "Estländisch-baltische Agrarentwicklung," in *Baltische Monatsschrift,* vol. 27, (1870), 143-151.
23. A. Bulmerinq, "Baltische Schragen," in *Baltische Monatsschrift,* vol. 6, (1862), 10.
24. G. Masing, "Über den Verkauf der Pastoralbauerlendereien," in *Baltische Monatsschrift,* vol. II, (1865), 205-239.

25. Heinrich Krummer, "Der Proletarier-Character der bäuer-lichen Ackerbau-Industrie in Liv-und Estland," in *Baltische Monatsschrift,* vol. II, (1860), 99-134.

Chapter III

1. "Saja aasta eest" (One hundred years ago), in *Eesti Kirjandus* (Estonian Literature), Tartu, I (1906), 6-9.
Paul Hunfalvy, *Reise in den Ostseeprovinzen Russlands,* Leipzig, 1874, 137-138.
2. "Saja Aasta eest," 8.
also: *Eesti Biograafiline Leksikon,* 432-433.
3. *Ibid.,* 433.
4. P. Hunfalvy, *op. cit.,* 137.
also: Gustav Suits, "Eesti Esiärkamise algus," (The begin-ning of Estonian pre-awakening), *Õpetatud Eesti Seltsi Aas-taraamat* (Yearbook of the Estonian Learned Society), of 1938, Tartu, 1940, 5-6.
5. A. Haselblatt, "Festrede zum 82ten Jahrestage der Gelehrten Estnischen Gesellschaft," in *Sitzungsberichte der Estnischen Wissenschaftlichen Gesellschaft,* Tartu, 1920, 136-137.
6. *Ibid.,* 138.
7. *Ibid.,* 138.
8. Hunfalvy, *op. cit.,* 138.
9. *Eesti Biograafiline Leksikon,* 1929, 572.
10. *Ibid.,* 572-73.
11. Harri Moora, Speech by, in *Õpetatud Eesti Seltsi Aastaraa-mat,* 1938, Tartu, 1940, 12.
12. P. Hunfalvy, *op. cit.,* 138-139.
13. "Veel Chr. J. Petersoin pildi puhul" (More about Ch. J. Peterson's picture), in *Eesti Kirjandus* (Estonian Literature) XI (1913), 428-429.
14. P. Hunfalvy, *op. cit.,* 139.
15. *Eesti Biograafiline Leksikon,* 1929, 96.
16. *Ibid.,* 97.
17. P. Hunfalvy, *op. cit.,* 139.
18. *Ibid.,* 139-140; also *Eesti Biograafiline Leksikon,* 1929, 96-98.
19. P. Hunfalvy, *op. cit.,* 139.
20. *Kalevipoeg,* by Friedrich Reinhold Kreutzwald, Toronto, 1954, 275-276.
21. William Forsell Kirby, *The Hero of Esthonia,* London, 1895, 142-143.

22. Gustav Suits, "Eesti esiärkamise alguse," (Beginning of Estonian awakening) in *Õpetatud Eesti Seltsi Aastaraamat*, (Estonian Learned Society 1938 Yearbook) 1938, Tartu, 1940, 6.
23. Harri Moora, *op. cit.*, 13-14.
24. *Ibid.*, 14.
25. *Ibid.*, 14.
26. Carl Schirren, *Livländische Antwort an Herrn Juri Samarin*, München und Leipzig, 1919, 190-193.
27. *Ibid.*, 15-16.
28. Paul Jordan, *Geschichte der ehstländischen literarischen Gesellschaft für die Zeit von 1842 bis 1892*, 32-36; 76-77.
29. *Eesti Biograafiline Leksikon*, *1929, 589-590*. The *Bibliatheca* was the basic bibliographical reference until after World War I.
30. *Ibid.*, 111
31. *Ibid.*, 572-575. See also page 72-73 above.
32. H. Rosenthal, *Kulturbesrebungen des esthnischen Volkes während eines Menschenalter,* Reval, 1912, 63.

Chapter V

1. [Alexander Buchholtz], *Fünffig Jahre Russischer Verwaltung in den Baltischen Provinzen*, Leipzig, 238-239.
2. H. A. von Bock, "Über den Handel auf dem Lande in Livland," in *Das Inland*, Vol. I, (December 16, 1836), Dorpat, 843-844.
3. *Ibid.*, 843-844.
4. *Ibid.*, Vol. II, (1837), 6.
5. "U." (author anonymous), "Die bäuerlichen Grundbesitzfrage," in *Baltische Monatsschrift*, vol. III, (January, 1861), 79-81.
6. *Ibid.*, 82.
7. Th. Böttischer, "Der Domainenverkauf in den Ostseeprovinzen und das Güterbesitzrecht," in *Baltische Monatsschrift*, January, vol. III, (1861), 399-400.
8. *Ibid.*, 424-425.
9. Jackson, *Estonia*, 99.
10. Böttischer, *op. cit.*, 424-425.
11. Bernard Uxüll zu Fickel, "Estländisch-baltische Agrarentwicklung," in *Baltische Monatsschrift*, vol. 27, (1886), 143-151. On page 150 the author writes: "Wo die Grossgrund-

besitzer diese Veränderung nur als eine Beschränkung ihrer Rechte und Befügnisse aufnahmen, wo sie infolge dieser gesetzlichen Befreiung der Gemeindeverwaltung von ihrem Einflusse, auch diesen Einfluss thatsächlich nicht mehr zu üben, Veranlassung zu haben glaubten, gab es Irrungen, Missverständnisse, Zwiespalt. Wo aber die Grundbesitzer in richtigem Verständniss des noblesse oblige, in richtigeme Verständnisses des Verhältnisses des Reicheren, des Gebildteren und der mit dem Selfgovernment vertrauten Klasse, and er Verwirklichung jener gesetzgeberischen Bestimmungen mitarbeiteten, da ist ein indirecter, beiden Seiten Günstiger Einfluss geübt worden . . ."

12. "U" (Anonymous) "Die Bäuerlichen Grundbesitzfrage," in *Baltische Monatschrift,* vol. III, January, (1861), 82.
13. *Ibid.,* 82.
14. *Ibid.,* 82.
15. "U.", Anonymous "Die bäuerlichen Grundbesitzfrage," in *Baltische Monatsschrift,* Vol. III, January, 1861, 82.
16. *Ibid.,* 83: "das der Gutsherr jetzt zur Überzeugung kommen müsse, dass das alte Band in seinen Grundfesten bereits wirklich gelöst ist und der Bauer sich eine eigenen selbstandige Hütte bauen müsse, der Gutsherr also soll zu bedenken habe, dass er einem freiem Menschen gegenuberstehe. Dieser freie Mensch steht aber auf der untersten Stufe der Bildung; unter seinen Stammesgenossen findet er keinen Halt; der zu einiger Bildung gelangter Theil der Nationalen tritt- mit sehr seltenen Ausnahmen-aus seinem Volke, von dem er durch Sprache, Sitte und Beruf sich scheidet heraus. Nur die Kirche bleibt ihnen noch gemeinsam, und auch hier nicht der Gottesdienst."
17. "E" (anonymous), "Das Volksschulwesen in Liv-Est-und Kurland," in *Baltische Monatsschrift,* vol. XXI, (1872), 538.
18. *Ibid.,* 546.
19. Gustav Suits, *Eesti Kirjanduslugu,* (History of Estonian Literature) Vol. I, Lund, 1953, 12.
20. *Ibid.,* 52; C. Parlo, J. Aavik, ja K. Mihkla, *Eesti Kirjanduslugu,* Heidenheim, (n. d.), 11.
21. *Ibid.,* 23-28; Gustav Suits, *Eesti Kirjanduslugu,* 76-111.
 * See Chapter IV.

Chapter VI

1. H. Rosenthal, *Kultur bestrebungen* etc., 37-38. See also: Gustav Suits, *Eesti Kirjanduslugu*, Lund, 1953, 183-192. *Eesti Biograafiline Leksikon*, Tartu, 1929, 166-170. Reinhard Wittram, *Baltische Geschichte*, München, 1954, 204-205.
2. Rosenthal, *op. cit.*, 38-39.
3. *Ibid.*, 40. Parlo, J. Aavik ja K. Mihkla, *Eesti Kirjanduslugu*, Heidenheim, (n. d.), 27; Gustav Suits, *Eesti Kirjanduslugu*, 86.
4. H. Rosenthal, *op. cit.*, 41-42: "Ein estnisches Volk mit dem Namen *Eesti rahvas* (Estonian people) existierte nicht. Die estnische Sprache war die der Bauern, das Volk, das diese Sprache sprach und für welches das Blatt geschrieben wurde, war ein Bauernvolk. Das war die allgemeine verbreitete, einzig gültige Anschaunng der damaligen Zeit."
5. See introduction.
6. H. Rosenthal, *op. cit.*, 45-46: "Dieser Auspruch ist daher grundlegend für die Erweckung des estnischen National bewusstseins. Durch denselben wird die Existenzeines estnischen Volkes konstantiert, das nicht einzig und allein auf eine Zahl von Bauern, besteht und darum ein armes, verachtetes Bauernvolk zu bleiben verurteilt ist, sondern das, ebenso wie jedes andere Volk, berechtingt sein muss, nach Bildung zu streben, höhere Kultur zu erlangen und seine Eigenart zu bewahren."
7. Rosenthal, *op. cit.*, 48-50.
8. *Eesti; Biograafiline Leksikon*, Tartu, 1929, 587.
9. H. Rosenthal, *op. cit.*, 54-58.
10. Rosenthal, *op. cit.*, 51, 73.
11. Gustav Suits, *Eesti Kirjanduslugu*, 216-224; *Eesti Biograafiline Leksikon*, 1929, 158-163.
12. *Eesti Biograafiline Leksikon*, 1929, 250-252.
13. *Ibid.*, 199-200.
14. *Ibid.*, 439-440.
15. H. Rosenthal, *op. cit.*, 73.
16. *Eesti Biograafiline Leksikon Täiendusköide*, 1940, 358-359.
17. Kristian Valdemars, *Über die Befehigung der Letten und Esten zum Seewesen*, and *Über die Heranziehung der Letten und Esten zum Seewesen*, both in 1857, Riga.
18. *Eesti Biograafiline Leksikon*, 1929, 359.
19. H. Rosenthal, *op. cit.*, 73.
19. *Ibid.*, 592.

20. Carl von der Recke, "Zur Beleuchtung der agrarischen Verhältnisse in den Ostsee-Provinzen," in *Baltische Monatsschrift,* vol. II, (1860), 323-335. In his article von Recke asserted that the main reason for the lack of improvement of
conditions among the Estonian peasantry was not the circumstance that they were renting the land, but the fact that
they still had to perform the vestiges of manorial labor. According to the author the moneyless peasants could not
afford to purchase the land they were tilling. Von Recke
therefore believed that, as a temporary solution, the peasants
should have stayed as long-term renters—an arrangement
which would induce them to improve their land and raise
their economic level.
21. Heinrich Krummer, "Der Proletarier-Character der bäuerlichen Ackerbau- Industrie in Livland und Estland," in *Baltische Monatsschrift,* vol. II, (1860), 104.
22. *Ibid.,* 105.
23. *Ibid.,* 105.

Chapter VII

1. R. Wittram, *Baltische Geschichte,* 188.
2. *Ibid.,* 188-189; 190-193.
3. "Offener Brief eines Balten an Geheimrath Katkov," in
Russisch-Baltische Blätter, (1887), 68-81.
See also: "Antwort auf die livländische Antwort des Herrn
Schirren," in *Livländische Beiträge,* vol. I (1870), 111-119.
4. J. Samarin, *Juri Samarin's Anklage gegen die Ostseeprovinzen Russlands,* translated and with an introduction by Julius
Eckard, Leipzig, 1869.
5. *Ibid.,* 43-46.
6. *Ibid.,* 49.
7. *Ibid.,* 53-58, 61-62.
8. *Ibid.,* 63-73.
9. *Ibid.,* 75-84.
10. *Ibid.,* 96-98; 106-107.
11. *Ibid.,* 112.
12. *Ibid.,* 113-119.
13. *Ibid.,* 130-131; 133-144.
14. Samarin, *op. cit.,* 145-162.
15. Carl Schirren, *Livländische Antwort an Herrn Samarin,*

München and Leipzig, 1919 (reprint from the original edition in Leipzig, 1869) 44; 136-137; 146-159.

16. *Ibid.*, 48-49.
17. *Ibid.*, 194.
18. "Estländische Korrespondenz," in *Baltische Monatsschrift,* vol. XXII, (1874), 69-84.
19. *Ibid.*, 55.
20. Anon., "Die Nationalitätenfrage," in *Baltische Monatsschrift,* vol. IX, (1864), 605.
21. *Ibid.*, 606.
22. *Ibid.*, 570.
23. Hans Kruus, "Turning-points of the Estonian National Awakening," in *Tartu Ülikooli Opetatud Eesti Selts* (Tartu University Estonian Learned Society), 1938, 193-195.
24. *Ibid.*, 196.
25. See pp. 131-133, this chapter.
26. H. Rosenthal, *Kulturbestrebungen,* 106-113.
27. Kruus, "Turning-points," 197-198.
28. *Eesti Biograafiline Leksikon,* 1929, 161; Gustav Suits, *Eesti Kirjanduslugu,* 1953, 224-243.
29. *Eesti Biograafiline Leksikon,* Tartu, 1929, 162.
30. *Ibid.*, 565.
31. *Ibid.*, 498-499; 525-527.
32. G. Suits, *op. cit.*, 192-205.
33. *Ibid.*, 225-243.
34. *Ibid.*, 209-215.
35. In his *Kolm Isamaa Kõned* (Three patriotic speeches), published in 1870, Jakobson described the six hundred years of German oppression as the Time of Darkness *(Pimeduse Aeg)* and after the emancipation, the Time of Light *(Valguse Aeg)*, terms which later became standard in Estonian historiography.
36. ". . . Man kann nicht nur . . . der Meinung sein dass die Kinder durch den Unterricht in der Muttersprache intensiver gebildet werden als durch einen sochen in einer fremden Sprache, sondern man kann auch der Ansicht sein, dass für das Estenvolk eine estnische Bildung die allein richtige sei. Diese Ansicht existiert factisch; und gegen diese Ansicht, scheint mir, kann man gar nichts haben. Das Estenvolk ist gewiss . . . berechtigt, Estenvolk zu sein und zu bleiben wie jedes andere Volk. Diejenigen nun, welche von diesem Standpunkt aus die Alexander-schule ansehen, reden von ihr in zweierlei Weise. Einestheils soll sie eine Zeugin sein des schon

so erstarkten estnischen Nationalgeistes, dass das Volk Leitung von fremder Hand abweisen könne; andererseits soll die Schule gerade die Emancipation des Estenvolkes von fremden Einflüssen zum Zweck haben and das nationale Bewusstsein des Volkes heben halfen. Ich kann auch in diesen Bestrebungen an sich nichts Unberechtigtes finden. Mag das Estenvolk eintreten in den Wettkampf der Nationen, mag es sich in der grossen Völkerarena einen Platz abstechen nehen den anderen Völkern, mag es die ihm von Gott gegebenenn Gaben ausbilden." L. Hörschelmann, "Die Estnische Alexanderschule und die Pastoren," in *Baltische Monatsschrift,* vol. XXVIII (1881), 675.

37. "E. B.," "Unsere Bäuerlichen Verhältnisse im Jahre 1871," in *Baltische Monatsschrift,* vol. XX, (1872), 600.
38. ". . . Der Aufruf hat die Bildung des Volkes im Auge und wir können ihm in soweit nur mit voller Überzeugung . . . zustimmen . . .". *Ibid.,* 600.
39. *Ibid.,* 606.
40. *Ibid.*
41. *Ibid.*
42. Die Nationalitätenfrage, in *Baltische Monatsschrift,* vol. IX, (1864), 566-575.
43. *Ibid.,* 570-572.

Chapter VIII

1. Theodor Pfeil, *Livlands Erlebnisse seit 50 Jahren,* Jurjew, [Tartu] 1906, 18-19.
2. *Ibid.,* 20-21; see also: "Lettisch-estnische Wandlungen," in *Russisch-Baltische Blätter,* Leipzig, (1887), 116-117.
3. Ado Grenzstein, *Herrenkirche oder Volkskirche? Eine estnische Stimme im baltischen Chor,"* Jurjev [Tartu] 1899, 123.
4. Johann Kõpp, *Mälestuste Radadel* (On the Roads of Memories), Lund, 1954, vol. II, 260-262.
5. *Eesti Biograafiline Leksikon,* 1929, 418.
6. Kõpp, *op. cit.,* vol. I, 194.
7. *Ibid.,* vol. II, 56-90; 143-158.
8. W. Lööralt, *Baltenhetze,* Leipzig, 1890, 1-12. Th. Pfeil, *Livlands Erlebnisse seit 50 Jahren,* Jurjev [Tartu], 1906, 9-10. See also chapter VII.

9. *Eesti Biograafiline Leksikon,* 1929, 299.
10. Villem Reiman, "Kolm ajaloohallikat venestamise päevilt" (Three historical sources from the Russification days), in *Eesti Kirjandus,* (Estonian Literature), 1910.
11. R. Wittram, *Baltische Geschichte,* 217-220.
12. *Die deutsche Universität Dorpat im Lichte der Geschichte und der Gegenwart,* Leipzig, 1882, 135-161.
13. Gustav Halber, "Über die gegenwärtige estnische Presse," in *Baltische Monatsschrift,* vol. LIV (1904), 141-152.
14. *Ibid.,* 152-158.
15. G. Halber, *op. cit.,* 158-162; see also: A. Grenzstein, *op. cit.,* 123-125.
16. A. Grenzstein, *op. cit.,* 4-9; 110-116.
17. *Eesti Biograafiline Leksikon,* 133.
18. *Ibid.,* 134.

Chapter IX

1. *Eesti Biograafiline Leksikon,* 1929, 537.
2. Michkel Martna, *Estland, die Esten und die estnische Frage,* Olten, (1919), 48-54; 57-61.
3. V. K. Jacunski, "Znachenie economicheskikh sviazei s Rossijei dlia khoziaistvennogo rasvitija gorodov pribaltiky v epokhu kapitalizma" (The importance of economic ties with Russia for the economic development of the cities of the Baltic provinces in the period of capitalism), in *Istoricheskie Zapiski,* (Historical Notes) vol. XLV (1954), 124-128.
4. "Anfänge der revolutionären Bewegung in Estland," in *Baltische Monatsschrift,* vol. LXI, (1906), 307-312.
5. *Ibid.,* 317-318.
6. Edward Laaman, *Konstantin Päts-Poliitka ja Riigimees,* (Konstantin Päts—politician and statesman), Stockholm, 1949, 11.
7. *Ibid.,* 13-16.
8. *Ibid.,* 20.
9. *Ibid.,* 21.
10. *Ibid.,* 21.
11. *Ibid.,* 23-24.
12. Ojamaa and Varmas, *Eesti Ajalugu,* 292-294.
13. *Eesti Biograafiline Leksikon,* 1929, 538.
14. *Baltische Chronik, 1903-1906,* Riga, 1906, 61.
15. *Ibid.,* 61.

16. *Ibid.*
17. *Ibid.*, 85.
18. *Ibid.*, 88.

Chapter X *

* All dates according to the Julian Calendar.
1. Ojamaa and Varmas, *Eesti Ajalugu,* 291-292.
2. *Eesti Biograafiline Leksikon,* 1929, 487-489.
3. *Baltische Revolutionschronik,* Riga, 1906.
4. *Baltische Revolutionschronik,* 50-56.
5. *Ibid.*, 6.
6. *Ibid.*, 70.
7. A. von Transche-Roseneck, *Die Lettische Revolution,* vol. II, Berlin, 1907, 399.
8. *Baltische Revolutionschronik,* 13-16.
9. *Ibid.*, 11-12.
10. *Ibid.*, 27.
11. *Ibid.*, 28-29.
12. Eduard von Dellingshausen, *Im Dienste der Heimat,* Stuttgart, 1930, 118-120.
13. Transehe-Roseneck, *op. cit.,* 398-400.
14. *Revaler Beobachter,* Reval Tallinn, August 21, 1905.
15. *Baltische Revolutions-Chronik,* 1905, 18.
16. *Ibid.*, 20; E. V. Dellingshausen, *op. cit.,* 114.
17. *Baltische Revolutions-Chronik,* 21.
18. *Ibid.*, 24.
19. *Ibid.*, 26.
20. *Ibid.*, 27.
21. Transehe-Rosenek, *op. cit.,* 221-225; *Baltische Revolutionschronik,* 1905, 31.
22. Eduard Freiherr von Stackelberg-Sutlem, *Ein Leben im baltischen Kampf,* München, 1923, 123-125.
23. *Ibid.*, 125.
24. Eduard von Dellingshausen, *op. cit.,* 112.
25. *Baltische Revolutionschronik,* 69.
26. *Ibid.*, 69-70.
27. Transehe-Roseneck, *op. cit.,* 400-402.
28. *Ibid.*, 402.
29. *Vorwärts,* Berlin, December 11-14.
30. Transehe-Roseneck, *op. cit.,* 221.
31. Eduard von Dellingshausen, *op. cit.,* 121-123.

32. *Ibid.*, 123-124.
33. *Baltische Chronik*, 1906, 185-187.
34. Quoted *ibid.*, 56, 64, 74.
35. Quoted *ibid.*, 74-75.
36. *Ibid.*, 165.
37. *Ibid.*, 171-174.
38. Michkel Martna, *Estland, die Esten und die Estnische Frage*, Olten, 1919, 29.
39. Georg von Rauch, *Russland-Staatliche Einheit und Nationall Vielfalt*, München, 1953, 145.
40. Astaf Alexander Georg von Transehe-Roseneck, *Die Lettische Revolution*, Berlin, 1907, part II, 399.
41. Alexander von Tobien, *Die Livländische Ritterschaft in ihrem Verhältnis zum Zarismus und russischen Nationalismus*, Berlin, vol. II, 215.
42. *Vorwärts*, Berlin, January, 1905-October, 1906.

Chapter XI

1. J. G. Kohl, *op. cit.*, 29.
2. *Ibid.*, 216.
3. Westren Doll, "Abgötterei zu Ausgang der schwedischen und Beninn der russischen Zeit," in *Sitzungsberichte der estnischen literarischen Gesellschaft, 1925*, 11-14: Where Catholic places of worship remained, the Estonians used them for secret meeting places, and during certain holidays (the birth of Mary), they brought sacrifices in the form of butter, eggs, cakes, money, and beer. Thursday was retained as a pagan holiday and observed in many villages.
The suppression of folk poetry continued into the first half of the nineteenth century, as one can see from the description of a contemporary German traveller, J. G. Kohl, who wrote that the German nobles and the pastors were continuing to chase out the old pagan habits from the Estonian mind. They forbade them to sing their folk songs and to tell their national tales, thus attempting to destroy the remnants of paganism. J. G. Kohl, *op. cit.*, 242-243.
4. Dr. Bertram (Pseudonym for G. J. Schultz), "Zur Geschichte und zum Verständniss der estnischen Volkspoesie," in *Baltische Monatsschrift*, vol. II, 1860, 431-433.
5. *Ibid.*, 440-448.
6. *Ibid.*, 433-434.

7. *Ibid.*, 431
8. "Livländische Korrespondenz," in *Baltische Monatsschrift,* vol. X, 1864, 273.
9. Oskar Loorits, "The Renaissance of the Estonian Nation," in *The Slavonic and East European Review,* vol. XXXIII, no. 80, December, 1954, 26.
10. M. Lipp-Nuggen, "Die Bedeutung des Dr. Schultz-Bertram für das estnische Volk," in *Sitzungsberichte der Estnischen Wissenschaftlischen Gesellschaft,* 1908, XXVIII-XXX.
11. Neubert, *Vom bedrängten Bruderstamm,* Dresden, 1906, 19-22.
12. G. C. Dehio, *Livland und Elsass,* Berlin, 1918, 16.
13. Friedrich Bienemann, *Babel über Acten,* Riga, 1880.
14. F. von Wrangell, *Die Russisch-baltische Frage,* Petersburg and Leipzig, 1883, 4-5.
15. *Ibid.*, 6-9.
16. Neubert, *op. cit.*, 26.
17. M. Martna, *Estland, die Esten etc.,* 18.
18. *Ibid.*, 17.
19. *Loc. cit.*
20. *Ibid.*, 17.
21. *Ibid.*, 18.
22. *Ibid.*, 18-19.
23. *Ibid.*, 20.
24. G. E. Luiga, *Die neue Agrarverfassung in Eesti,* Dorpat, 1924, 7.
25. "Z," (Unknown), *Das baltische Problem und die Vorschlage zur seiner Losung,* Reval, 1906, 20.
26. *Loc. cit.*
27. M. Martna, *op. cit.*, 8-9.
28. *Vorwärts,* Berlin, January-October, 1905.
29. *Baltische Monatsschrift,* vol. LVIII, 1950, 120.

BIBLIOGRAPHY

A. PRIMARY SOURCES

I MEMOIRS, REMINISCENCES, TRAVEL ACCOUNTS

Anon., *Ausflug nach Ehstland im Januar, 1807*, (n.p.), 1830
Anon., *Ausflug nach Ehstland im Junius, 1807*, Meiningen, 1830.
Paul Hunfalvy, *Reise in den Ostseeprovinzen Russlands*, Leipzig, 1874.
Johann Georg Kohl, *Die deutsch-russischen Ostseeprovinzen oder Natur und Volk-erleben in Kur-, Liv- und Estland*, Dresden und Leipzig 1841, vol. I, II.
Johan Kopp, *Mālestuste Radadel*, (On the Road of Memories) I, 1953, II, 1954, Lund.
Heinrich Rosenthal, *Kulturbestrebungen des estnischen Volkes wahrend eines Menschenalters* (1869-1900), Reval, 1912.
Edward von Dellinghausen, *Im Dienste der Heimat*, Stuttgart, 1930.
Eduard Freiherr von Stackelberg-Sutlem, *Ein Leben im baltischen Kampf*, München, 1923.

II CONTEMPORARY WORKS OF POLITICS AND SOCIAL CRITICISM

Baltische Revolutions—Chronik, Oktober-December, 1905, 2 vol., Riga, 1907-1908.
Friedrich Bienemann, *Babel über Acten*, Riga, 1880.
Kaspar Biezbardis, *Der Sprach—und Bildungskampf in den baltischen Provinzen*, Bauzen, 1865.
Herman Bruiningk, *Livländische Rückschau*, Dorpat, 1879
[Alexander von Buchholz], *Fünfzig Jahre russischer Verwaltung in den Baltischen Provinzen*, Leipzig, 1883.
Deutsch-Protestantische Kämpfe in den baltischen Provinzen

Russlands, Leipzig, 1888.

G. G. Dehio, *Livland und Elsass,* Berlin, 1918.

Sopie Dehio, *Reval einst und jetzt,* Reval, 1910.

Julius Eckardt, *Die baltischen Provinzen Russlands,* 1869, Leipzig.

————, *Bürgerthum and Bürokratie,* Leipzig, 1870.

R. J. L. Samson von Himmelstierna, *Historischer Versuch Über die Aufhebung der Leibeingenschaft in den Ostseeprovinzen,* 1838.

Carl Robert Jakobson, *Offene Antwort des Herausgebers der "Sakala" auf das Zweite Anlageschreiben des pastors Hurt,* Fellin, 1879.

Heinrich von Jannau, *Geschichte von Lief- und Ehstland pragmatisch vorgetragen,* Riga, 1893.

W. Lööralt, *Baltenhetze,* Leipzig, 1890.

Michkel Martna, *Estland, die Esten, und die estnische Frage,* Olten, 1919.

Garlib Merkel, *Die Letten vorzüglich in Liefland am Ende des philosophischen Jahrhunderts,* Leipzig, 1800.

Heinrich Ferdinand Mühlau, *Die Ostseeprovinzen Russlands und ihre deutsche Kultur,* Kiel, 1906.

(v. Neander) *Die Deutsche Universität Dorpat im Lichte der Geschichte und der Gegenwart,* Leipzig, 1882.

Nash Ostzeiski Vopros (Our Eastern—See Question), Leipzig, St. Petersburg, (n. d.).

K. H. Neubert, *Vom bedrängten Bruderstamm,* Dresden, 1906.

Theodor Pfeil, *Livlands Erlebnisse seit 50 Jahren,* Dorpat, 1906.

Gystav von Rennenkampf, *Bermerkungen über die Leibeigenschaft in Liefland und ihre Aufheburg,* Kopenhagan, 1818.

The Revolution in the Baltic Provinces of Russia, ed. by Ernst O. F. Ames, London, 1907.

Juri Samarin, *Okrainy Rossii,* (Russia's Borderlands) Praga, 1863.

Russische Semstvo und baltische Selbstverwaltung, Theodor von Schiemann, ed., Leipzig, 1878.

Carl Schirren, *Livländische Antwort an Herrn Juri Samarin,* Leipzig, 1919.

L. von Würstemberger, *Die Gewissensfreiheit in den Ostseeprovinzen Russlands,* Leipzig, 1872.

III OFFICIAL DOCUMENTS

J. H. Gressel, ed., *Ehstländische Bauern-Verordnungen*, Reval, 1816.

————————, *Ehstländische Bauern-Gesetzbücher*, Reval, 1816.

————————, *Gesetzbuch für die ehstländischen* Bauern, Reval, (about 1804).

IV COLLECTED SOURCES

Baltische Briefe aus zwei Jahrhunderten, Alexander Eggers, compiler, Berlin, 1919.
Sbornik materialov i statei po istorii Pribaltiiskogo Kraia, vol. I, (Collection of sources on the history of the Baltic region), Riga, 1876.

V PERIODICALS AND SERIES PUBLICATIONS

Baltische Monatsschrift, Riga, Reval, 1859-1939.
Beiträge zur Kunde Estlands, vol. 1-8 1873-1915, Reval.
Õpetatud Eesti Seltsi Aastaraamat (Yearbook of the Estonian Learned Society), Tartu, 1940.
Russisch-Baltische Blätter; Beiträge zur Kenntnsiss Russlands und seiner grenzmarken, Erstes Heft, 1886, Zweites Heft, 1887, Drittes Heft, 1887; Viertes Heft, 1888, Leipzig.
Vorwärts, Berlin, January, 1905-October, 1906 (Daily)

VI REFERENCE WORKS

Allgemeine Deutsche Biographie, Leipzig, 56 vol., 1875-1912.
Evald Blumfeldt and Nigolas Loone, *Eesti Ajaloo Bibliograafia* (Estonian Historical Bibliography), MOCCC-LVVVII, 1933-1, 1939, Tartu.
Bolshaia Entsiklopediia, St. Petersburg, 22 vol., 1900-1909.
Eesti Biograafiline Leksikon, (Estonian biografical lexicon), vol. 1 1929, Tartu.
Eesti Biograafiline Leksikon, Täienduskoide, Tartu, 1940. (Estonian biografical lexicon, additional volume)

VII

Friedrich Reinhold Kreutzwald, *Kalevipoeg,* Toronto, 1954.
Gustav Suits, *Flames in the Wind,* a selection from the poetry of,
[Introduction by] W. K. Matthews, London, [1953].

PERIODICALS AND REFERENCE WORKS USED AT THE UNIVERSITY OF MUNICH (GERMANY)

Das Inland, Dorpat, 1800-1837.
Livländische Beiträge, edited by Woldemar von Beck, Berling, 1867-
Entsiklopedicheskii Slovar' (Encyclopaedical Dictionary), edited by I. C. Andreevskii, St. Petersburg, 1890-1907, 41 vol., 2 supplementary volumes.
G. W. Lewitzki, *Biographical dictionary of the professors in the University of Dorpat,* 1802-1902, Dorpat.
J. F. Recke, K. E. Napiersky, *Allgemeiner Schriftsteller und Gelehrten-Lexicon der Provinzen Livlands, Ehstlands, und Kurlands,* 4 volumes, Mitau, 1827-1832.
Theodor Reise and others, *Allgemeiner Schriftsteller und Gelehrten-Lexikon,* I-II, Mitau, 1859-1861.
Rigasche Biographien, 3 volumes, Riga, 1881-1884.

VIII ARTICLES

Adolf Agthte, "Ursprung und Lage der Landarbeiter in Livland," in *Zeitschrift für die Gesammte Staatswissenschaft,* Tubingen, 1909, Heft, XXIX.
Karl Ast-Rumor, "Gustav Suits—tänane unelus" (Gustav Suits—today's dream) 322-325, *Tulimuld,* nr. 6, 1952, Lund, Sweden.
J. Aunver, "Johan Kõpp 80-aastane" (Johan Kõpp 80 years old), 258-263, *Talimuld,* nr. 5, 1954.
E. F. Duciuk, "Krestianjkie dvizhemia v Livonii v vtoroi polovine 18-ovo Veka," (Peasant movements in Livonia during the second half of the 18th century), *Istoricheskie Zapiski,* (Historical Notes), vol. XIII, 1942, Moscow.
M. J. Eisen, "Eesti rahva Kasvamine," (The growth of the Estonian people) 49-58, *Eesti Kirjandus* (Estonian Literature), II, 1910, Tartu.

"C. R. Jakobsoni kirjad J. Adamsonile," (C. R. Jakobson's letters to J. Adamson), *Eesti Kirjandus*, nr. 7, 1913, 268-282.

"C. R. Jakobsoni kirjad professor Johan Köhlerile," (C. R. Jakobson's letters to professor Johan Köhler), *Eesti Kirjandus*, nr. 1, 1913, 29-32. nr. 2, 1913, 77-83.

"C. R. Jakobsoni kirjad Mart Mittile" (C. R. Jakobson's letters to Mart Mitt), *Eesti Kirjandus*, VI, 1906, 173-179.

"J. W. Jannseni Kirjad tsensor M. Suigusaarele," (J. W. Jannsen's letters to the censor M. Suigusaar) 126-129, *Eesti Kirjandus*, III, 1912.

Michkel Kampman, "C. R. Jakobson kui padagog," (C. R. Jakobson as an educator), 97-104, *Eesti Kirjandus*, III, 1912.

Hans Kruus, "Turning-points of the Estonian national awakening," in *Tartu Ülikooli Õpetatud Eesti Selts*, 1938, Tartu. (Tartu University Estonian Learned Society).

"Kurzer Uberlick auf die Russificirung der Ostseeprovinzen," in *Russisch-Baltische Blätter*, Leipzig, 1887, 52-69.

"Lettisch-Estnische Wandlungen," *Russisch-Baltische Blatter*, Leipzig, 1887, 115-135.

Oskar Loorits, "The Renascence of the Estonian Nation," in *The Slavonic and East European Review*, vol. XXXIII, nr. 80, December, 1954.

Jaan Luiga, "Noor- Eesti II," (Young Estonia), *Eesti Kirjandus*, I, 1907.

Charles Leonard Lundin, "The Road from tsar to kaiser: changing loyalties of the Baltic Germans, 1905-1914," *Journal of Central European Affairs*, vol. 10, nr. 3, October, 1950.

"Mineviku material ja Mõned kirjad Eesti Kirjameeste Seltsi lõpu päevilt," (Material from the past and some letters concerning the final days of the Estonian Literary Society), *Eesti Kirjandus*,

Willem Reiman, "Kolm ajaloohallikat venestamise päevilt," (Three sources concerning the days of Russification), *Eesti Kirjandus*, 104-116, III, 1912.

"Saja aasta eest" (Hundred years ago), *Eesti Kirjandus*, I, 1906, 6-16; II, 1906, 33-45; III, 1906, 65-79; IV, 1906, 99-103; V, 1906, 129-139; VI, 1906, 161-172; VII, 193-213.

J. Sitska, "Kuidas orjus meile tuli" (How we got into slavery), *Eesti Kirjandus*, nr. 1, 1917, 1-11, Tartu.

Gustav Suits, "Fr. R. Kreutzwald ta elulojakul" (Fr. R. Kreutz-wald's life) *Tulimuld*, 426-439, nr. 6, 1951.

Ilmar Talve, "Eesti kultuuriajaloo probleeme" (Estonian Cultural and historical problems), 204-210 *Tulimuld*, nr. 4, 1952. 259-261, nr. 5, 1952.

"Noor Gustav Suits Soomes" (The young G. Suits in Finland) 1901-1911, Tulimuld, nr. 6, 1953.

Uluotsa, "Professor Jüri mälestusraamat" (Professor J. Uluots' commemorative book), Stockholm, 1945.

J. W. Weski, "Eesti Kirjanduse Seltsi tegevus ja kavatsused" (The activities and plans of the Estonian Literary Society), *Eesti Kirjandus*, nr. 5-6, 1914, 137-146, Tartu.

B. SECONDARY SOURCES

I BOOKS

Leonid Arbusow, *Ocherk istorii Lifliandii, Estlandii, i Kurliandii*, (Outline-History of Livland, Estonia and Courland), St. Petersburg, 1912.

Richard Bahr, *Volk Jenseits der Grenzen, Hamburg* 1933.

Christian August Berkholz, *Die sieben Jahrhunderte Livlands von 1159-1859*, Riga, 1860.

Friedrich Bienemann, *Aus baltischer Vorzeit*, Leipzig, 1870.

————, *Die Katastrophe der Stadt Dorpat während des Nordischen Krieges*, Reval, 1902.

Alfred Bilmanis, *Baltic Essays*, Washington, D. C., 1945.

Arnold Raphael Cederberg, Die Erstlings der estländischen Zeitungsliteratur in, *Acta et Commentationes Universitatis Dorpatensis*, Vol. II, Tartu, [about 1930].

Carl Croeger, *Geschichte Liv-, Ehst- und Kurlands*, 2 vols., St. Petersburg, 1867-1870.

Die deutschen Ostsee-provinzen Russlands, Geschichtlich, Kulterell und Wirtschaftlich dargestellt von Kennern der Baltischen Provinzen, Theodor von Schiemann, editor, Berlin, 1918.

Die deutsche Universität Dorpat im Lichte der Geschichte und in der Gegenwart, 1882, Dorpat.

Julius Wilhelm Albert von Eckardt, *Baltische und russische Cultur-studien aus zwei Jahrhunderten*, Leipzig, 1869.

————, *Livland im 18ten Jahrhundert*, Leipzig, 1876.

Alexis Freiher von Engelhardt, *Die deutschen Ostsee-Provinzen, ihre politische und wirtschalthche Entwickenng*, München, 1916.

Axel von Gernet, *Die im Jahre 1802 eröffnete Universität Dorpat und die Wandlungen in ihrer Verfassung*, Reval, 1902.

Rheinhold von Holstein, *Baron Hamilkar von Fölkersahm*, Riga, 1907.

John Hampden Jackson, *Estonia*, London, 1941.

Paul Jordan, *Geschichte der ehstländischen literarischen Gesellschaft fur die Zeit von 1842 bis 1892*, Reval, 1892.

Hans Kruus, *Grundriss der Geschichte des estnischen Volkes*, Tartu, 1932.

Zildonis Ligers, *Geschichte der baltischen Städte*, Bern, 1948, (also in French).

Otto Liiv, *Die wirtschaftliche Lage des estnischen Gebietes am Ausgange des XVII Jahrhunderts*, Tartu, 1935.

Georg Edward Luiga, *Die Agrar-reform in Eesti, ihr Werdegang und ihr Wesen*, Helsigfors, 1920.

————, *Die Neue Agrarverfassung in Eesti, ihre Geschichtlinien, Ursachen und sozial-politischen Auswirkungen*, Dorpat, 1925.

Constantin Mettig, *Baltische Städte*, Riga, 1901.

M. Ojamaa-A. ja T. Varmas, *Eesti ajalugu*, (Estonian History), Stockholm, 1946.

O. Parlo, *Eesti kirjanduslugu* (History of Estonian literature), Heindenheim, 1947.

Georg von Rauch, *Russland- Staatliche Einheit und Nationale Vielfalt*, München, 1953.

A. von Richter, *Geschichte der dem russischen Kaiser-reiche einverleibten deutschen Ostseeprovinzen*, Riga, 1857-58.

Helmut Speer, *Das Bauernschulwesen im Gouvernment Estland am Ende des Achtzehnten Jahrhunderts bis zur Russifizierung*, Tartu, 1936.

Gustav Suits, *Eest Kirjanduslugu*, (History of Estonian Literature), vol. I, Lund, 1953.

Gustav von Stryk, *Das Agrargesetz in Livland* (Lettland und Estland), Dorpat, 1922.

————, *Die Landwirtschaft in Livland*, Dorpat, 1918.

204   Estonia: *Nation on the Anvil*

Tartu, Tartu Linna-Uurimise Toimkonna Korraldatud ja Toi-
metatud, Tartus, 1927. (Tartu, Arranged and edited by the
City-research-editorship).
Tartu, Resume Francais, 1927.
Tartu, (Dorpat), Deutsches Referat, 1928.
Alexander von Tobien, *Die Agrargesetzgebung Livlands in 19ten
Jahrhundert,* Berlin, 1881.
Jüri Uluots, *Grundzüge der Agrargeschichte Estlands,* Tartu,
1935.
Johan Vasar, *Eesti majandus vene ajal XIX sajandi keskpaigani,*
(The Estonian economy during the Russian period until the
middle of the nineteenth century). Tartu, 1937.
Die Vereinigung des Ostseegebiets mit Russland, E. B. von
Tiesenhausen, preface, editor, Riga, (1869).
Friedrich Wiegand, *Siebenhundert Jahre Baltischer Kirchen-
geschichte,* Gütersloh, 1921.
A. Winkler, *Aus der Früzeit des estlandischen Zeitung-swesen,*
Reval, 1929.
Reinhard Wittram, *Baltische Geschichte, Die Ostseelande Liv-
land, Estland, Kurland,* 1180-1918, Munchen, 1954.
————, *Meinungskämpfe im baltischen Deutschtum während
der Reformepoche des 19ten Jahrhunderts,* Riga, 1934.
————, *Rückkehr ins Reich,* Posen, 1942.

C. SPECIAL WORKS

Eduard Laaman, *Konstantin Päts,* Stockholm, 1949.

INDEX

Aleksandri-Kool (Alexander School), 99, 101, 102, 103, 104, 107, 117, 138.
Alexander I (Tsar), 21, 29, 30, 31, 40.
Alexander II (Tsar), 86, 91, 93, 97, 99, 101, 115.
Alexander III (Tsar), 103, 111, 115, 157.
All-Estonian Congress, 151.

Baltische Monatsschrift, 53, 110.
Bebel, A., 157.
Bellegarde, A., 130, 142.
Bibliotheca Livonia Historicae, 68.
Blumberg, G., 100.
Brest-Litovsk, 170.
Browne, Y., 24.

Catherine the Great, 15, 24, 94.
Creditkassen, 98.

Dellinghausen, Baron von, 130, 131.

Eisen, v. Schwarzenberg, J. G., 16, 19, 20, 27.
Emancipation Bill, 30.
Estonian Communist Party, 172.
Estonian Diet, 30.
Estonian Learned Society, 57, 58, 59, 62, 66, 67, 99, 100, 160, 161.
Estophilism, 61, 67, 76.

Fählman, F. R., 57, 58, 59, 60, 61, 62, 64, 67, 77, 91.
Fölkersahm, H. von, 45.
Frey, P. H. von, 55.

Ganander, C., 60.

German Lutheran Church, 111, 119.
Goltz, von der, 170.
Great Northern War, 13, 21, 22, 23, 30.
Grenzstein, A., 118, 119, 120, 123.
Grewingk, C. C., 68.
Grimm, J., 160.
Güldenband, U., 115.

Hahn-Postenden, T. von, 51.
Harju, 46.
Hegel, G., 128.
Herder, J. G., 20, 59.
Hermann, K. A., 113, 120, 123.
Himmelstierna, S. von, 45.
Hollmann, F. A. W., 48.
Holtz, O. R. von, 55.
Hupel, A. W., 17, 18, 20, 27, 160.
Hurt, J., 68, 85, 99, 100, 102, 103, 104, 105, 106, 114, 120, 128, 162.

Igaüks (Everybody), 22.

Jaakson, J., 127.
Jakobson, C. R., 86, 87, 91, 99, 102, 103, 105, 106, 114, 118, 119, 120, 162.
Jannau, H. von, 16, 19, 20, 27, 30, 38.
Jannsen, J. W., 80, 81, 82, 83, 84, 86, 87, 88, 89, 91, 99, 102, 105, 106, 110, 114, 115, 120, 123, 128, 162.
Järv, J., 118, 120.
Jung, J., 68.
Jurjev, A., 86, 87.
Jürgenstein, A., 156.

Kadakasaksad, 7, 34, 83, 168.

Kalevala, 58, 62.
Kalevipoeg, 59, 61, 62, 65, 160, 163.
Kallas, O., 123.
Kapustin, M., 116.
Karell, P. J., 86, 87.
Katkov, M. N., 93, 115, 161, 163.
Kerensky, A., 170.
Knüpffer, A. F. J., 55.
Koidula, L., 105.
Kohl, J. G., 32, 33, 39.
Köhler, J., 86, 87, 102.
Koppel, H., 123.
Kõpp, J., 115, 156.
Kõrv, J., 113, 117, 120.
Kordt, A., 85.
Kreutzwald, F. R., 59, 60, 61, 64, 67, 68, 69, 77, 91, 102, 163.
Kruus, H., 99, 101.
Kuhlbars, F., 105.

Laakman, A., 81, 82.
Laidoner, J., 171, 173.
Landeswehr, 170.
Landes-Verwaltung, 138.
Leipziger Volkszeitung, 125.
Lettophils, 20, 21.
Livonian Diet, 30, 51.
Lopukhin, A., 142.
Luce, J. W. L. von, 55, 57.
Luiga, G. E., 148.
Luig, A., 85.
Lutheran Church, 25, 39, 43, 44, 115, 163.

Maarahva Postimees (The Peasants' Mailman), 81, 82.
Mahtra, 46.
Manassein, N., 115, 116.
Martna, M., 148.
Masing, O. W., 55, 57, 58, 61, 81.
Merkel, G., 18, 19, 20, 27, 30, 38, 57.
Meyer, L., 68.
Mielberg, J., 85.
Molotov-Ribbentrop Pact, 177.

Moravian Brethren, 25, 27, 76, 160.
Moravian Churches, 26.
Moravian Movement, 50.
Moskovskaia Gazeta (Moscow Gazette), 93.
Mythologia Fennica, 60.

National Liberal Party, 134, 150, 151.
National Socialist German Workers Party, 174.
Nicholas I (Tsar), 44.
Nicholas II (Tsar), 145.
Noor Eesti (Young Estonia), 169.
Nordlivländische Zeitung, 132, 133.
Novoye Vremya (New Era), 154.
Nystad, 13.

Obram, A. F., 85.
Okrainy Rossii (Russia's Borderlands), 94.
Olevik (The Present), 119, 120.

Parts, K., 156.
Patkull, J. R., 61.
Pärno Postimees (The Pärno Mailman), 81, 82.
Päts, K., 126, 127, 129, 131, 135, 136, 142, 148, 149, 170, 173, 174, 175, 177.
Patriotic League, 174.
Paul (Tsar), 94.
Peter the Great, 14, 40, 94.
Peterburger Zeitung, 155.
Peterburgas Awises (Petersburg Gazette), 86, 87.
Peterson, K. J., 59, 60, 67, 76, 77, 91.
Philaret (Bishop), 43.
Poska, J., 148, 170.
Pold, P., 156.
Postimees (The Mailman), 120, 126, 128, 129, 132, 134, 135, 136, 141, 142, 147, 156.
Proudhon, P. J., 127.

Pung, M., 148.
Püha Seltsirahvas (Holy Brotherhood), 160.

Reiman, V., 114, 123, 128, 162.
Ritterschaften, 36, 130.
Revaler Beobachter (The Reval Observer), 143.
Rosenplänter, J. H., 55, 56, 60, 61.
Russian Academy of Science, 58.
Russian Orthodox Church, 35, 42, 43, 44, 70, 94, 111, 126, 153, 154, 161.
Russow, N. F., 86.

Sakala, 102, 103, 118.
Samarin, J., 93, 94, 95, 96, 115, 161.
Samson-Urbs, H., 89.
Sannumetoja, 81.
Schirren, C., 66, 67, 96, 99, 161.
Schoultz, K. F., 19, 20, 27, 163.
Schwarzenberg, J. G. E. von, 16.
Seerni Laulukannel, 80.
Sirk, A., 173, 174.
Slavophils, 96, 97.
Smetona, A., 175.
Social Democratic Party, 143, 145, 153.
Social Revolutionary Party, 143, 151, 157.
Sõnumeid (News), 113.
Sööt, K. E., 156.
Speek, P., 136, 142, 151.
Stackelberg-Sutlem, E. von, 148.
Stimmen der Völker, 160.

Taara, 147, 148.
Tartu University, 57, 59.
Teataja (The Announcer), 126, 129, 130, 135, 136, 168.
Teemant, J., 147, 148, 151.
Teutonic Knights, 30, 32, 38.
Thol, G., 82.
Tõnnisson, J., 123, 124, 126, 129, 131, 133, 134, 135, 141, 145, 146, 147, 150, 155, 156, 157, 173.
Treffner, H., 104.

Ugannia, 147.
Ulmanis, K., 175.
Ungarn-Sternberg, Baron, 40.
Uudised (News), 132, 136, 142, 147.

VABS, 173, 174, 175.
Valdemars, K., 86, 87.
Valgus (Light), 113, 118.
Vanemuine, 84, 127.
Virulane (The Vironian), 118.
Vorwärts (Forward), 157.

Walter, F. (Bishop), 47.
Weske, M., 68, 102, 103, 105, 162.
Wiedemann, F. J., 58, 59, 68.
Willigerode, A. H., 81, 82, 84.
Winkelmann, E., 68.
Witte, S. I., 153.

Yrjö-Koskinen, Y. S., 69.

Zimse, J., 47.
Zinzendorf, 25.